Cartographical Curiosities

Cartographical Curiosities

GILLIAN HILL

THE BRITISH LIBRARY

Contents

© 1978, The British Library Board
ISBN 0 904654 42 7
Published by the British Library
Reference Division Publications
Great Russell Street, London WC1B 3DG

 British Library Cataloguing in Publication Data

Hill, Gillian
Cartographical curiosities.
1. British Library. Map Library
2. Maps — Exhibitions.
I. Title   II. British Library
016.912   GA190.L/

Designed by John Mitchell
Set in 9/11 Century
Printed in Great Britain by
G A Pindar & Son Ltd, Scarborough

Introduction

Maps need not always serve a wholly geographical purpose. They may be literary, satirical, frivolous, or simply decorative. The fertile imagination of map-makers has contorted the countries of the world into human and animal shape, created allegorical lands of vice and virtue, and invented new realms for the characters of fiction to walk in. Maps have appeared in strange disguises, as jigsaw puzzles, playing cards, or political cartoons. The aim of this booklet is to draw attention to some of the more unusual maps in the British Library, whether based on genuine geographical misconceptions or the deliberate whimsy of cartographers.

The booklet has been written by Gillian Hill. Sarah Tyacke contributed the section 'Maps and Myths' and provided notes on the religious items. The selection of maps described in the booklet is based on that made for the exhibition 'Cartographical Curiosities' mounted by the British Library Map Library in April 1978. The Department of Manuscripts kindly lent maps **35, 36, 61** and **73**.

The British Library Board gratefully acknowledges the loan of items from the following:

Mr Dudley K. Barnes (**86**)
The Bodleian Library (**45**)
The Guardian (**77**)
The Hannas Collection (**10, 11, 15, 18, 19, 84**)

Mr Raymond O'Shea (**82, 83, 85**)
The executors of the late Professor J. R. R. Tolkien (**31**)
Mr Peter Walne (**85**)

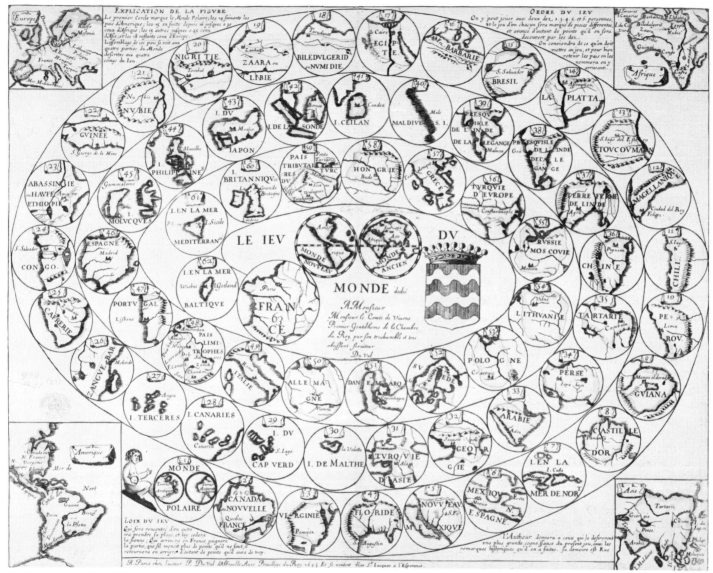

1   *Le jeu du monde, 1645*

TABLE GAMES

Many an indulgent Victorian mama, attempting to make the study of geography a little less dull for her numerous offspring, might have been somewhat taken aback to discover that the educational game she was purchasing was a thinly disguised version of a traditional French gambling game, the 'jeu de l'oie': a game of chance, popular on the Continent since the Middle Ages, and by no means unknown in English inns. In this 'game of goose' a number of players, each represented on the board by a marker of a distinctive colour or shape, pursue one another along a set track, moving onwards from square to square according to the throw of the dice. Various hazards may be met with on the way, these being traditionally marked by the figure of a goose; the first player to overcome them all and reach the final square is the winner, and collects all the stake-money. Different manufacturers over the years have introduced a wide variety of elaborations and complexities, and an even wider variety of pictorial boards, but the familiar *Snakes and Ladders* principle is always lurking in the background.

The earliest board games in the Map Library are all French. First in the field is *Le Jeu du Monde* of 1645 (1), which is an example of the simplest form of the 'jeu de l'oie'. The track consists of 63 circles arranged in an anti-clockwise spiral, working inwards from the bottom left-hand corner of the board. Each circle contains the map of a country from one of the four known continents, the final and winning circle showing France. From two to six people may play, using two dice; the only rules are (a) that a player throwing a greater number than is necessary to reach the final circle must 'rebound' by the amount of the excess, and (b) that if a player's throw takes him to a circle already occupied by another, the two change places. The spice of gambling is nicely mixed with a touch of instruction in a single sentence: 'On conviendra de ce qu'on doit mettre au jeu, et pour bien retenir les pais on les nommera en y arrivant'—name the stakes, and name the countries. Except for this slight educational element, the maps are not really relevant to the game; but their presence is not surprising, for the game was invented by Pierre du Val, 'Geographe du Roy'. He was a prolific map-maker whose output included several games during the second half of the seventeenth century. Twenty-five years after the *Jeu du Monde*, in 1670, he produced *Le Jeu des Princes de l'Europe* — a very similar game, but rather more elaborate. It is again a spiral of 63 circles, decorated with maps, but there are also forfeits, with ransoms and fines to be paid. As well as his original stake, a player who lands on certain numbers must pay the same sum into the pool, the eventual winner collecting all the money. 'Celui qui arriuera en la petite Tartarie payera rançon plus tost que de se laisser mener Esclaue a Constantinople' — any player landing on 'la petite Tartarie' (circle 57) must pay ransom, to avoid being taken to Constantinople as a slave. He must also return to the beginning of the track. Du Val also produced in 1652 an attractive draughtsboard, *Le Jeu de France pour les Dames* (2). Instead of being alternately black and white, as on the traditional board, the squares are mapped or blank — 32 of them are quite plain, the other 32 contain small maps of the different regions of France.

In England, although variations of the 'game of goose' were certainly known, it was only towards the end of the eighteenth century that printed 'board-games' began to be published to any great extent. (They were not in fact issued on boards, but on paper mounted on canvas or linen.) The first known dated game is *A Journey through Europe*, produced by the geographer John Jefferys in September 1759. This was to

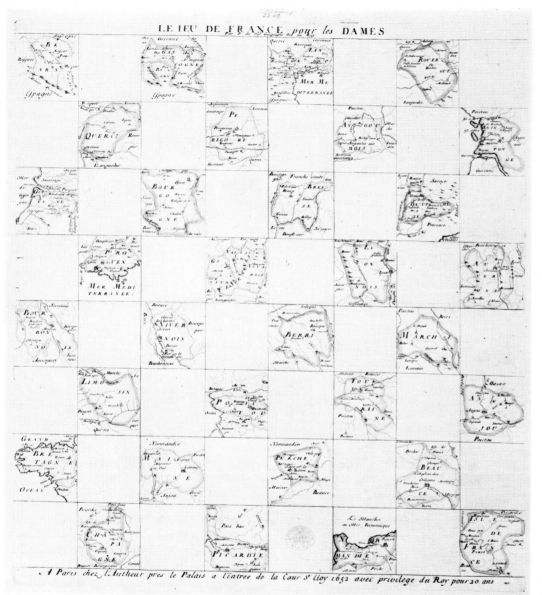

2   *Du Val's draughtsboard, 1652*
3   *The Royal Geographical Pastime, 1770* ▶

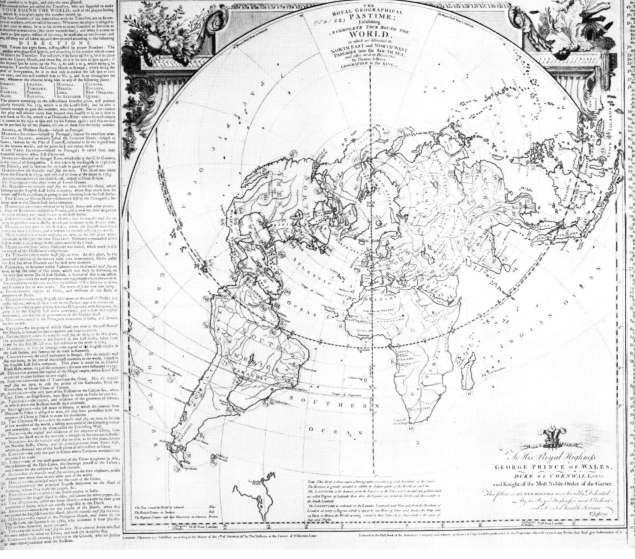

THE
ROYAL GEOGRAPHICAL
PASTIME:
Exhibiting
A COMPLETE TOUR ROUND THE
WORLD
in which are delineated the
NORTH EAST and NORTH WEST
PASSAGES into the SOUTH SEA,
and other modern Discoveries.
By Thomas Jefferys
GEOGRAPHER to the KING.

To His Royal Highness
GEORGE PRINCE of WALES,
DUKE of CORNWALL, &c.
and Knight of the Most Noble Order of the Garter.
This Plate is BY PERMISSION most humbly Dedicated
By his Royal Highnesses most Obedient
and Devoted humble Servant
T. Jefferys.

set the pattern for map games for the next eighty years, although it seems to have been over a decade before the idea was first copied by anyone else. Then in January 1770 Thomas Jefferys (apparently unrelated) produced *The Royal Geographical Pastime: Exhibiting a complete tour round the world in which are delineated the North East and North West Passages into the South Sea, and other modern Discoveries* . . . (**3**), and a companion game with a tour of England and Wales. In these three games, and many of their successors, the geometrical arrangement of the course has been replaced by a track meandering across the surface of a map, punctuated by numbered stopping-places at various cities or other places of interest. A descriptive list of these stopping-places accompanies the game, sometimes mentioning only those that carry forfeits or bonuses, but more often including every place along the route, with a sentence or two describing each, to be read out by any player landing on that number. In the earlier games these lists are usually type-set and pasted down either side of the engraved map; later they appear in separate accompanying booklets. The *Royal Geographical Pastime* covers 103 stopping-places from the Azores to Land's End:

'77. PATAGONIA — *here the traveller must stay one turn,* to see the supposed race of giants, with which we have been lately amused.'
'99. BAHAMA ISLANDS — . . . *the traveller . . . will be shipwrecked on these islands, and lose his chance for the game'.*

It is common for some disaster to occur near the end of the course, forcing the traveller to retire from the game. In this version he is never entirely out of danger, for if he overshoots Land's End he must return to the 'Oroonoko River', no. 89, and brave the Bahamas again. If, however, he lands on no. 58, he may take advantage of the North-West Passage and go straight to no. 79 — Cape Horn.

The move of the race-game from the inn to the family fireside was taking place in a context of changing attitudes to education. People were beginning to realize that although children had to be educated, there was no reason why learning should be tedious, and that children might even absorb information more readily if lessons were made enjoyable. For the first time books were being published specifically for children; works which were instructional or moralistic, but amusing too. The opportunity was there for enterprising publishers to find new ways of combining instruction with entertainment, and maps had obvious possibilities. They already had an established place in the schoolroom, and being graphic had an advantage over grammar-books or arithmetical tables when it came to making them more attractive to the young pupil. So the old gambling games were toned down and adapted to become educational toys. By the end of the eighteenth century the games had been adapted for many other subjects, history and biblical stories among others; but however attractive the pictures on the board, no other subject has ever adapted to the race-track quite as well as geography.

One way in which the old games were made respectable was by the removal of the dice, with all their dubious connotations. Instead, the extent of a move was decided by spinning a teetotum. This is a kind of top, with numbered sides; when it comes to rest, the player moves his piece according to the number that is uppermost. The teetotum, or 'totum' as it was also known, could have any even number of sides. Eight seems to have been most common, but it could sometimes be six, like a die, or as few as four or as many as twelve. Some games specify 'the totum must be marked 1 to 8 on its several sides, with pen and ink', suggesting the use of a home-made teetotum; it was easy enough to construct, by cutting an octagonal piece of card, numbering it, and pushing a thin stick through the middle as a pivot for spinning. Otherwise the teetotum would probably be made of bone, as would the other necessary bits and pieces (**10**). Players were represented on the board by 'pillars' or 'travellers', looking not unlike small pawns from a chess-set. Small counters, often known as 'markers' or 'servants', were also used for various purposes. Each player would have four of these 'servants' of the same colour as his 'traveller'; on reaching a square where he was instructed to 'wait three turns' he would deposit three of his 'servants', picking up one each time it would normally have been his turn to move, until he had a full complement again, when he could rejoin the pursuit. In the nineteenth century these counters were often quite elaborately carved from mother-of-pearl.

The areas most often depicted in race-games were England and Wales, the world, and Europe — these being the areas the children most often had to consider. Different publishers varied the rules slightly, according to individual fancy — usually in such minor points as what a player should do if he overshot the final square. One pub-

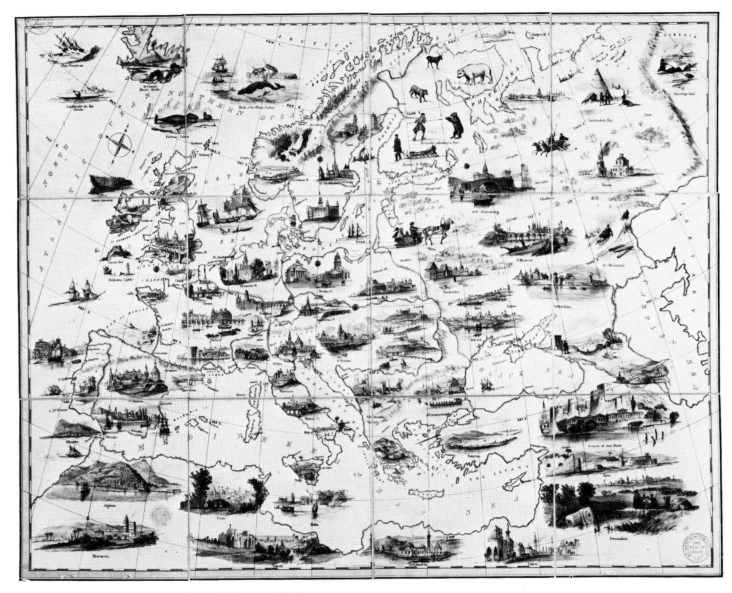

6   *The Travellers; or, A Tour through Europe, 1842*

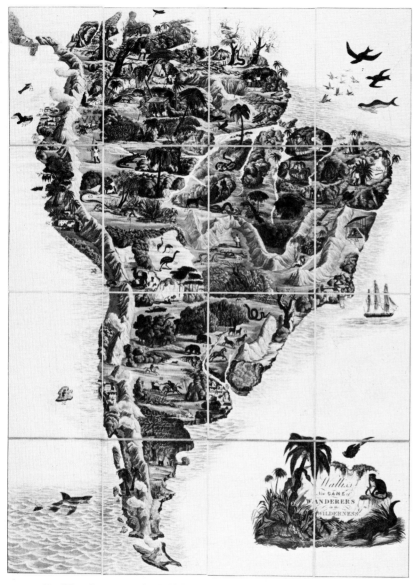

lisher, Robert Sayer, in his *New Royal Geographical Pastime for England and Wales* (1787), made such a player return to square one, which must have lengthened the game considerably. Sayer was one of the few who did not use a consecutive numbering system for the race-track, but jumped from town to town at random. This meant the player had to work out what number to proceed to, then check the list at the sides to discover what town was indicated — so if he did not know where the town was on the map, he could not move his 'traveller'. A little hard on the young, perhaps, but probably more effective than most games at teaching geography.

For the most part, however, the publishers of these games were not so adventurous, and kept closely to the original pattern. *Wallis's Tour through England and Wales* (4), produced by John Wallis of 16 Ludgate Street in 1794, follows the familiar formula, as does his son Edward's *Wallis's New Railway Game* (5) over forty years later. Both have a 117-stop track, running from Rochester to London; in both the player may be shipwrecked at no. 89, the Isle of Man. The two games are in fact identical; Edward has merely taken the plate engraved for his father's game, and added railways to it, in an attempt to take commercial advantage of the 'railway mania' of the time. The rules have been reset in a more modern type-face, and slightly altered, giving prominence to towns which happen to have railway stations. 'New Railway Game' is a misnomer, for the game is neither new nor about railways; although they appear on the map, they have no significance in the game, and the route of the race-track completely ignores them. Edward Wallis saw the commercial possibilities of the railways for his business, and saved himself time, money and trouble by adapting his father's old copper plate rather than creating a new game. The descriptions of the towns have been only slightly altered from the first version, where they include such intriguing information as:

'87. *Appleby* — the County Town, tho' but an inconsiderable place'.
'79. *Halifax* — a considerable town, and is the great market for shalloons, callimancoes, everlastings, &c'.

By the middle of the nineteenth century, the appearance of the map-games was at last beginning to change. The early ones had been engraved on copper plates, as were all maps, and painstakingly coloured by hand; now the advent of chromolithography made colour

7   Wanderers in the Wilderness, c.1845

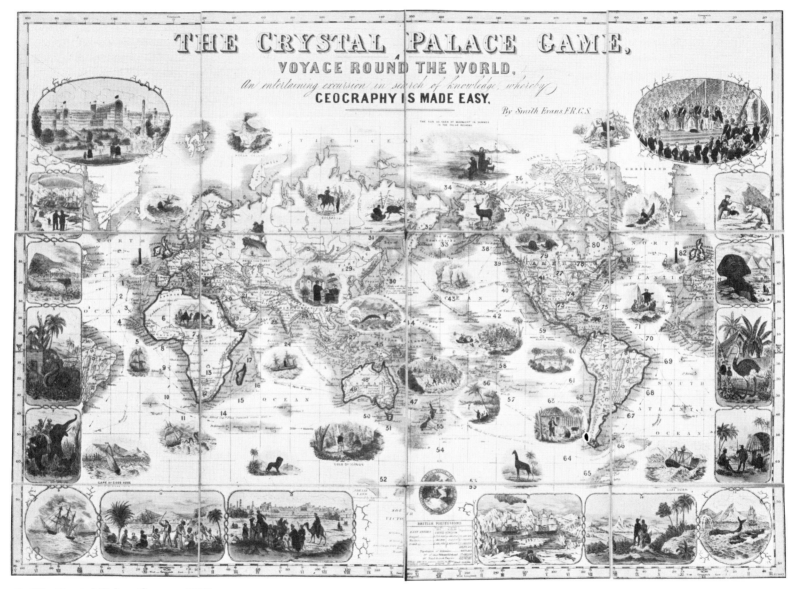

8   *The Crystal Palace Game, c.1854*

printing not only possible but cheap, though it was still common to find hand-colouring used for the finer detail. Map-games ceased to be the simple affairs they had been for so long, with little more than rivers, towns and boundaries marked on them; they acquired colourful views and scenes, inset at appropriate places.

William Spooner's *The Travellers; or, a Tour through Europe* (6) is an early example of the gaudier games. It is a colourful map of Europe, with charming little scenes scattered over it. Most are views of the architectural masterpieces of the various European cities, but towards the north the artist has run out of famous buildings and shows instead 'a Finlander attacking a Bear', or a 'Russian & Sledge'. It is not one of the conventional tour games; up to five people may play, each starting from a different point, and moving north, south, east or west along the parallels as indicated by the teetotum.

At about the same time, Edward Wallis produced a series of highly decorative games. One of the most exotic was *Wanderers in the Wilderness* (7), in which the players are invited to imagine themselves exploring the wilds of South America. The accompanying list no longer describes towns and cities but the flora and fauna of the jungle:

> '42. Hark! there is danger near! Do you not hear the warning of the Rattle Snake? See how his fiery eyes glare on that poor bird:- it hops and flutters nearer and nearer to his destroyer, till it drops fairly into his mouth. — *Draw quickly another number,* lest you be the next victim, for his bite is mortal'.

Instead of a teetotum, Wallis now supplied numbered pieces of card, to be drawn from a bag.

The Crystal Palace Game, a voyage round the world, An entertaining excursion in search of knowledge, whereby geography is made easy (8), was obviously inspired by the building of the Crystal Palace for the Great Exhibition of 1851. Designed with an extremely decorative map, the board also displays fourteen colourful scenes around the edges — 'Nelson when a Midshipman killing a Bear', 'Tiger Hunt in India' and others in the same vein. The booklet provides not only the usual descriptive list of places visited — at the Antipodes the player is 'at liberty to turn two summersaults, by way of exemplifying the revolutions of the Globe' — but also a page of useful advice on the cost of the voyage:

> 'All Provisions, Wine, Spirits, and Sugar being shipped 'duty free,' — the cost of living on board would be much less than on shore. Contracts could be made to supply the Sailors with provisions, &c., according to an agreed *dietary table* from 10d. to 1s. per diem, and the Cabin Passengers, including Wine, &c., at 3s. 6d. to 5s'.

From the middle of the nineteenth century onwards, cheap colour printing made all kinds of games increasingly widely available. Dice became respectable again, and the trappings of the games grew more elaborate, as model ships or cars replaced the simple 'pillars'. The educational bias gradually decreased, although it has never disappeared. Map games form a smaller portion of the market than they once did, but the geographical element is still important in games today, from the complexities of *Diplomacy* to the strange diagram of the *Monopoly* board.

DISSECTED PUZZLES

The same conditions that favoured the development of the table-game also created an appropriate background for the invention of what we now know as the jigsaw puzzle. At the time of the publication of John Jefferys's *Journey through Europe* in 1759, a young man called John Spilsbury was nearing the end of his apprenticeship with Thomas Jefferys, who would later produce map games of his own. By the early 1760s Spilsbury was in business by himself, and producing 'dissected maps' as well as the more usual variety in one piece. He would mount a map on a thin piece of mahogany, then cut it up into a number of pieces, so that children might learn their geography by putting it together again.

Spilsbury's *The World* (11) of c.1772 is typical of the early puzzles, though on different wood. The pieces do not interlock; the map is cut up along the borders of the different countries, the sea being cut at random in rather larger pieces. From an educational point of view, this geographical method of cutting was obviously a good idea; the child would remember both the shape of the country and its whereabouts in the world. Where map table-games were essentially toys, albeit of an educational nature, dissected maps would sometimes be used in the schoolroom itself, perhaps as light relief after some more arduous task. The educational uses of the puzzles were stressed in advertisements:

12 A New Map of Africa, dissected

16 Middlesex on a playing-card

Bowles and Carver's new and enlarged Catalogue of 1795, includes

'BOWLES's *Dissected Maps,* pasted on wood, and accurately cut out into their respective kingdoms, states, provinces, counties, &c. in order to unite the various separated parts of each map together again, which imprints on the mind their situation, extent, &c. Designed for the use of schools, and for teaching young Ladies and Gentlemen the Geography of the World, or any particular part thereof, in an easy and entertaining manner. Each Map is contained in a neat square mahogany box. Price 7s 6d. each; or dissected of a larger size, including the whole of the sea-coasts and degrees. Price 10s 6d. each'.

One interesting feature of the advertisement is that the map puzzle could be bought more cheaply without the sea. Spilsbury had introduced this idea and others had also adopted it. Comic as it seems at first, it was sound business sense; it saved both time and materials to cut roughly round the edge of England and Wales, ignoring the surroundings. These puzzles, being produced economically, could be sold more cheaply, thus widening the market for an otherwise rather expensive item. Other dissected puzzles could not of course be treated in the same way. Spilsbury himself is not known to have produced any dissections other than maps, but within a few years of the publication of his invention competitors were producing a variety of puzzles. As with table-games, the alternative subjects are often of an instructional or improving nature — chronological tables of the kings and queens of England, or illustrations of moral tales. Despite this variety, map dissections retained a very substantial share of the market — Bowles and Carver's 1795 *Catalogue* lists ten available maps, but only six other puzzles.

The first puzzles were cut from mounted copies of existing maps and prints. As the demand increased, some publishers produced designs especially for dissection, and sometimes included the cutting-lines on the engraving. Others preferred not to limit their copper plates to a single use in this way, and continued to dissect designs which could also be sold separately as prints. There are at least two examples of the Wallis family using copies of their board-games to produce dissected puzzles, thus providing the purchaser with a bonus of two games for the price of one. In 1812, incidentally, John Wallis was claiming to have invented the dissected puzzle thirty years previously.

An early development in the cutting of the puzzles was the introduction of the interlocking frame. Puzzles were not made fully interlocking until the beginning of the twentieth century, when a die was introduced for cutting the whole picture at once, but it was realized early on that a reasonably firm frame was a great advantage when putting a puzzle together. This can clearly be seen in *Pilgrim's Progress Dissected* (24), produced by John Wallis in 1790, and later in Darton's 1818 *New Map of Africa* (12). These puzzles are far from complicated by today's standards. The map of Christian's journey from *Pilgrim's Progress* is made up of only thirty pieces, while the large puzzle of Africa has forty-five pieces, averaging just over ten square inches each! By contrast the picture-map jigsaw of *Shakespeare's Country* (13), produced by Francis Chichester not long after the Second World War, has 210 fully interlocking pieces of less than one square inch each. This puzzle also harks back to the mid-nineteenth-century race games, being accompanied by an informative guidebook giving descriptions of the forty-two places pictured on the map.

'In every age since its foundation Oxford has produced its quota of world-famous scholars, statesmen and administrators. On a less exalted plane, its gifts to civilisation include Cooper's marmalade, and Morris' motor cars'.

Today the great majority of puzzles are pictorial, from the vast ones of over 2000 pieces down to the popular dissected postcards. As with board-games, the educational bias of the jigsaw is greatly diminished; map puzzles are still published, but their heyday is long past.

PLAYING-CARDS

Playing-cards are a gambling device which one might not at first expect to find adapted to educational uses. Special cards have been designed at various times for particular games, educational or otherwise, but the familiar 52-card pack has always been more appropriate to amusement than to improvement.

The first playing-cards were doubtless very simple, but by the middle of the fifteenth century highly decorative ones were being produced on the Continent. It seems to have been some time before anyone chose to adorn them with maps, but in 1590 'W.B.' (William Bowes) had the happy thought that the number of counties in England and Wales corresponded exactly with the number of cards in the traditional English pack. He produced four printed sheets, each comprising the fifteen cards of a suit, although bearing no distinguishing suit-marks. The extra cards were an introductory card and a card of doggerel verse, which could be laid aside when the sheets were cut up for play; they were presumably included because it is far easier to fit fifteen items to a sheet than thirteen. Each of the fifty-two main cards has a square central panel bearing a small map of one of the counties, and a number from I to XIII in the top left and bottom right corners. The spaces above and below each carry four lines of text describing the county.

Early in the seventeenth century Bowes produced another pack in which county maps form a small part of an exceedingly intricate design, but after these no further such cards are known until those published by Robert Morden in 1676. He grouped the suits in very much the same way as Bowes had done, by area, but did not follow his system of giving the smallest county in a suit the lowest number. The layout of the individual cards is also similar: the map again appears in a square panel in the centre. In the top section is the name of the county, with the number of the card on the left in small arabic numerals and on the right in large Roman numerals. There is space on the left for the addition of a suit-mark. The court cards bear a head in a circle on the right: the king and queen are recognisable as Charles II and his consort Catherine of Braganza, but the knaves are different for each suit and do not appear to be specific portraits. The third section of each card gives statistical information concerning the county illustrated. In 1680 a later edition of this pack was sold bound as an atlas, entitled *A Pocket Book of all the Counties of England and Wales*. In about 1773 H. Turpin reissued the cards as *A Brief Description of England and Wales* (16). In this atlas the cards are pasted opposite a descriptive text, which gives the history of the various counties and details of market towns, rivers, products and seats (of country gentlemen, not Members of Parliament). In this form the playing-card has become useless to the gambler, and finds a place in the schoolroom or library after all.

20a *Stokes's Capital Mnemonical Globe collapsed*

A common feature of the nineteenth-century schoolroom was the globe. A good one could be extremely expensive, and various attempts were made to produce acceptable cheap alternatives. One variation on the traditional sphere was *Mogg's Dissected Globe* (**18**), produced in 1812. It was not strictly speaking 'dissected', as it had never been a single item in the first place; in common with dissected maps, however, it had to be put together. Four shaped pieces of pasteboard, printed with maps, were placed upright and held together by a series of interlocking horizontal circular pieces representing the equator, the tropics and so forth, the whole device, when complete, having the general shape of a globe and stand. The various pieces carry much useful information, but it can scarcely have been usable as a globe when constructed.

A rather more practical collapsible globe was produced by John Betts, a major publisher of dissected puzzles and other educational items, in about 1852. His *Portable Globe* was made up of eight gores, linen-backed for strength, and joined along the line of the equator. This could be packed flat, or made to form an approximate sphere by pulling the two drawstrings linking the points of the gores at the North and South Poles. The result would be rather flimsy, and not geometrically exact, but a reasonable substitute for a rigid globe.

This system was also used by one William Stokes, Teacher of Memory. In 1868 he published *Stokes's Capital Mnemonical Globe* (**20**), 'by which the relative positions of the principal geographical places in the world may be learned as an amusement in a few hours'. In addition to all the usual countries and oceans, this globe is possessed of a face. The idea is that one can more easily recall the precise position of a place on the globe by relating it to something with a well-known configuration — in this instance, the human head. Once one has memorised the basic feature of the system, that the Greenwich meridian runs straight down the centre of the nose, Greenwich itself being roughly in the middle of the forehead, one can locate, for instance, the Cape Verde Islands by remembering that they are at the inner corner of the right eye. Indeed, Mr. Stokes suggests that 'a little playful pleasantry . . . will enliven the proceedings, and . . . strengthen mental impressions'. He encourages the use of mnemonics such as 'Europe, on the centre of the forehead, *you're up*', and ends his introduction to the use of the globe with the somewhat optimistic comment, 'every head we look at supplies us with a gratuitous and unwitting exercise in geography'.

20b Stokes's Capital Mnemonical Globe expanded

22 *Utopia*

2 The Realms of Fiction

'The Ilande of Utopia conteyneth in breadthe in the myddell part of it (for there it is brodest) CC miles. Whiche bredthe continueth through the moste parte of the lande. Sauyng that by lytle and lytle it commeth in, and waxeth narrower towardes both the endes. Whiche fetchynge about a circuite or compasse of v.c. myles, do fassion the hole Ilande lyke to the newe mone. Betwene thys two corners the sea runneth in, divydyng them a sonder by the distance of xi miles or there aboutes, and there surmounteth into a large & wyde sea . . . The forefrontes or frontiers of the ii corners, what wythefordys & shelves, & what with rockes be very ieoperdous & daungerous. In the middel distaunce betwene thē both stādeth up aboue the water a great rocke, which therfore is nothing perillous bicause it is in sight. Upō the top of this rocke is afaire & a strōg towre builded'.

Sir Thomas More's Utopia is probably the most famous of all invented countries, even among those who have never heard of its author; it is one of the few which have passed into everyday imagery, in company with Lilliput and Ruritania. The *Utopia* was first published in 1516 and, unlike many later works set in imaginary lands, it provides a clear description of the fictitious topography. The island is shaped like a crescent with points curving inwards to within eleven miles of each other, leaving a vast inland bay protected at the mouth by rocks and shoals, with a watchtower built upon the largest rock. The width of the body of the crescent is about 200 miles, narrowing towards the ends, and the overall circumference of the island is 500 miles. Straightforward as this description appears, the country cannot be mapped. If a circle has a circumference of 500 miles, its overall diameter must be less than 160 miles — so a width of 200 miles for the greater part of the crescent is clearly impossible. The first edition of the *Utopia,* published at Louvain in 1516, is illustrated with an anonymous woodcut showing a perspective view of the island. It reaches a reasonable compromise;

the island is circular, with a large bay guarded by a tower, although it could scarcely be described as crescent-shaped. Two years later the third edition was published in Basel, this time with a woodcut (**22**) attributed to Ambrosius Holbein, elder brother of Hans. As a work of art it is greatly superior to that in the first edition; as a representation of the island, however, it is noticeably inferior. Holbein appears to have adapted the first woodcut, without any reference to the text. Thus the overall shape is similar, but important details have been altered: the bay has gone, leaving the island a simple circle (although the watchtower remains); and the mouth of the island's main river, clearly labelled as such, is no longer anywhere near the coast. In so far as the river reaches the sea at all, it appears to do so at its source.

With many writers, the inconsistency of the description could safely be assumed to arise from failure to attend to detail. In the case of Sir Thomas More, it seems more likely that it was deliberate. He takes great care in the text of the book to show that the island does not actually exist. 'Utopia' itself means 'nowhere', the river 'Anydrus' means 'no water', and other place-names and personal names are also nonsensical; it is quite plausible that he should describe the island in a way which not only shows it to be non-existent but makes it unmappable.

The allegorical landscape of the travels of Christian in *The Pilgrim's Progress* (**24**), first published in 1678, is easier to map. There is little general description, but the various stages of Christian's journey are detailed in full, from his departure from the City of Destruction to his safe arrival at the Celestial City. The straight and narrow road leads him through such places as the Valley of the Shadow of Death and Vanity Fair, while off to one side or other along the way lie the distractions and temptations he must contend with. Thus the basic scheme of the route is fairly clearly defined, but the individual cartographer still

has considerable licence to make of the countryside what he will.

The exact position of the island of Utopia is never revealed, and Christian's travels take place in an admitted dream world. The countries visited by Swift's insatiable traveller, Lemuel Gulliver, however, can often be located to within a few thousand miles. The second book of his *Travels* (**25**), published in 1726, describes his involuntary visit to Brobdingnag. His ship is caught in a fearful storm, 'so that the oldest Sailor on Board could not tell in what part of the World we were'. On 16 June 1703 land is sighted, and on the following day Gulliver is one of the landing-party. By chance he is left alone in this strange country, and finally gleans enough knowledge of the place to work out roughly where he is.

> 'The whole Extent . . . reacheth about six thousand Miles in Length, and from three to five in Breadth. From whence I cannot but conclude that our Geographers of *Europe* are in a great Error, by supposing nothing but Sea between *Japan* and *California*; for it was ever my Opinion, that there must be a Balance of Earth to counterpoise the great Continent of *Tartary*; and therefore they ought to correct their Maps and Charts, by joining this vast Tract of Land to the North-west Parts of *America*, wherein I shall be ready to lend them my Assistance'.

Communication with the rest of North America is prevented by a range of volcanoes, thirty miles high, across the neck of the peninsula. Gulliver's description of the interior of the country, however, is of less use to the map-maker. He is more concerned with the social institutions of the inhabitants, and gives only incidental details relevant to the topography of the country.

Trollope's Barsetshire, on the other hand, suffers from an excess of local topographical information. The general picture of the countryside is fairly clear, but contradictions abound in the detail. Ronald Knox brought these to light when he attempted to map the county in 1922 (**26**), more than fifty years after the novels were written. At the beginning of the first of the Barsetshire novels, *The Warden,* the cathedral is at the west end of Barchester, but in the later novels it has moved eastwards, and stands by the London Road. Similarly, the distance between Barchester and Plumstead shrinks from nine miles in *Barchester Towers* to less than five in *The Last Chronicle of Barset*. The railway, too, has its idiosyncrasies: it passes within a mile and half of Courcy, which is a considerable way from its route. Trollope cannot be credited

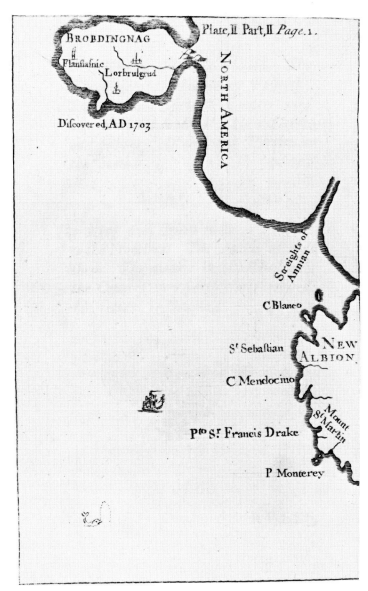

25 *Brobdingnag*

27 *Treasure Island*

with Sir Thomas More's motives for deliberately making his creation unmappable. It seems more probable that, while keeping a general view of the county in his mind, he invented the details at random to suit the particular chapter he was writing, without checking whether he had already invented a conflicting detail elsewhere.

This method of writing would scarcely have suited Robert Louis Stevenson, who believed 'the author must know his countryside, whether real or imaginary, like his hand; the distances, the points of the compass, the place of the sun's rising, the behaviour of the moon, should all be beyond cavil'. It was a belief he practised himself: if Utopia is the most famous invented country, 'Treasure Island' (**27**) must surely be the most famous map in English literature. Yet it was not originally drawn to illustrate a book; rather, the book was written to illustrate the map. In the summer of 1881 Stevenson was staying in 'the Late Miss McGregor's Cottage' in Braemar, confined to the house by a combination of ill-health and bad weather. His stepson, Lloyd Osbourne, spent much of the holiday occupied with his paint-box, and sometimes Stevenson would join him. 'On one of these occasions, I made the map of an island; it was elaborately and (I thought) beautifully coloured; the shape of it took my fancy beyond expression; . . . I ticketed my performance 'Treasure Island'.' Then, 'as I paused upon my map of 'Treasure Island', the future character of the book began to appear there visibly among imaginary woods . . . The next thing I knew I had some papers before me and was writing out a list of chapters'. And so the book was born. Stevenson found that parts of his story were almost written for him by the map: he had casually labelled an islet 'Skeleton Island', and to explain this he introduced 'Flint's pointer', the skeleton of a buccaneer from Captain Flint's crew, laid out to mark a compass bearing. 'And in the same way, it was because I had made two harbours that the *Hispaniola* was sent on her wanderings with Israel Hands'.

Unfortunately, while the manuscript was with the publishers, it was discovered that the map had been lost. To publish the book without it was unthinkable, so Stevenson had to sit down and go through the entire process in reverse. 'It is one thing to draw a map at random, set a scale in one corner of it at a venture, and write up a story to the measurements. It is quite another to have to examine a whole book, make an inventory of all the allusions contained in it, and with a pair of compasses, painfully design a map to suit the data. I did it; . . . but somehow it was never *Treasure Island* to me'.

Not all treasure maps are as straightforward as Stevenson's. At the end of the seventeenth century it was believed locally that shipwrecked Spaniards had buried considerable amounts of treasure on the island of Ireland in the Bermudas, and certainly a few items of Spanish silver had been found there. In 1693 the surveyor John Rowe went out and took a number of bearings from the sites of objects thought to be markers left by the Spaniards, but the results were inconclusive. The following year William Hack drew the map of Ireland (**61**), and copied Rowe's notes.

> '. . . and because of these pointings, a Spanish Silver Spoon & a turtle shell box inlayed with silver being found between the Bolt & yellow-wood tree, people doe imagine they hid their treasure on that narrow part of Ireland, some fantcy in the great Cave a strange & great place (but small entrance) these Reports & the sight of the places, moved my curiosity to sett Spanish point from the ends of Ireland with my Semicircle with graduates & I found its situation as layd down but its form is Imaginary'.

Children's books remain one of the richest sources of imaginary lands. Often the localities are complete inventions, as with C. S. Lewis's Narnia, but others are adaptations of reality — the Lake District of Arthur Ransome's *Swallows and Amazons* (**30**), or *Pooh Corner* (**29**), 'drawn by me and Mr. Shepard helpd', based on the area around Cotchford Farm in Sussex, where the Milnes lived. Even the youngest readers are catered for, with *The Rev. W. Awdry's Railway Map of the Island of Sodor, where Thomas the Tank Engine and his friends live and work* (**32**). Sodor, an old collective name for the Isle of Man, the Hebrides and other islands west of Scotland, is represented as an island several times larger than the Isle of Man, lying in the Irish Sea between Douglas and Barrow.

In J. R. R. Tolkien's *The Hobbit* (1937), a map is again a crucial part of the story rather than mere illustration. Thorin, the leader of the dwarves, is given a map of the Lonely Mountain made by his grandfather Thror many years earlier. There are runes on the map describing a secret entrance to the mountain, but it is not until the party reaches the Last Homely House that further 'moon-letters' are discovered, explaining how to find the key-hole of the secret door. These 'moon-letters' are runes written with a silver pen, and can only

"What's the good of Mercator's North Poles and
  Equators,
Tropics, Zones, and Meridian Lines?"
So the Bellman would cry: and the crew would
  reply
  "They are merely conventional signs!

"Other maps are such shapes, with their islands
  and capes!
But we've got our brave Captain to thank"
(So the crew would protest) "that he's bought us
  the best——
A perfect and absolute blank!"

This was charming, no doubt: but they shortly
  found out
That the Captain they trusted so well

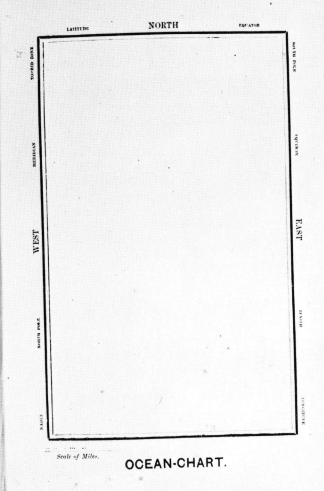

OCEAN-CHART.

be seen by holding the map up to a moon of the same phase and season as the one under which they were written. Tolkien originally drew 'Thror's Map' (31) with these runes on the verso, so that they could only be read if it was held up to the light. He had hoped that it could be printed thus, on the two sides of a leaf at the appropriate place in the volume, but the publishers preferred to transfer the runes to the front of the map and print it as an endpaper. Tolkien also drew working sketch-maps for the later works *The Lord of the Rings* and *The Silmarillion;* those in the published volumes were by his son Christopher.

All the maps so far described have been associated with the work of individual authors. Bernard Sleigh's *Anciente Mappe of Fairy Land newly discovered and set forth* (33) knows no such limitations. The 'mappe' is a colourful panorama, over six feet long, which illustrates every myth, legend, fairy story, children's fantasy and nursery rhyme the author could think of. Old Mother Hubbard, Tom Piper and Miss Muffet all live in the same row of terraced cottages, with Humpty Dumpty watching them from a wall across the road. Behind them Little Boy Blue is sleeping not far from Red Riding Hood's House, which stands at the foot of Avalon. Peter Pan's house is just across the sea from Valhalla, and Ulysses' Shippe is passing the rock where they blow the Horns of Elfland. This curious jumble of traditions is not wholly successful. In particular the legends of Scandinavia and of Greece and Rome do not mix happily with relatively modern fiction: the ancient stories are too closely associated with specific localities to seem at home in a fairy land of complete fantasy.

Two regions that do not appear to have been mapped are Wonderland and Looking-Glass Country, although it might be said that any chessboard is an adequate map of the latter. Lewis Carroll does, however, provide a chart for his readers in *The Hunting of the Snark* (34). It is a reproduction of the one purchased by the Bellman, organiser of the expedition and captain of the ship:

> 'He had bought a large map representing the sea,
>   Without the least vestige of land:
> And the crew were much pleased when they found it to be
>   A map they could all understand'.

Not, admittedly, one of the most decorative maps in fiction, but a memorable one nonetheless.

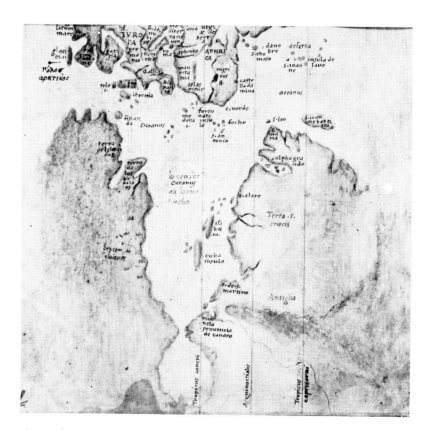

35 *Atlantic islands, c.1508*

3 Maps and Myths

It is perhaps paradoxical that as various parts of the world became better known and others were newly discovered from the fifteenth century onwards the geographical legends of earlier and classical times were not discarded. They either retreated further into the unknown interiors of continents or were transmuted into a more modern guise. The new continent of America existed side by side in men's minds with a belief in legendary islands and unicorns. Shakespeare's Moor of Venice told Desdemona his 'travells Historie', which encompassed not only 'hils whose heads touch heaven' but also 'the Cannibals that each other eate; the Anthropophagie, and men whose heads doe grow beneath their shoulders'.

One such example of transmogrification is that of the legendary islands of the Atlantic, which remained on maps even with the discovery of America after Columbus's landfall in the West Indies in 1492. The islands recalled earlier journeys of explorers such as St Brendan of Ardfert who sailed into the Western Ocean in search of a Land of Promise sometime during the sixth century AD. Later expeditions by the Spaniards and Portuguese from their settlements in the Canaries and Azores also sought undiscovered islands on the western fringes of the ocean, notably the islands of Antilla and of Seven Cities (*Septem Civitates*) which had been shown on seamen's charts since 1424. As late as 1487 a Portuguese fleet set sail to find these islands.

On a map of the Atlantic in an atlas of sea charts usually attributed to Vesconte Maggiolo of Genoa and drawn about 1508, the fusion of new American discoveries and legendary island place-names is neatly illustrated (**35**). St Brendan's Fortunate Islands lie next to Madeira in the Azores, while the known islands of the West Indies lie off the coast of the mythical *Antiglia* (Antilla) and *Terra S. Crucis,* first called South America in 1507 after Amerigo Vespucci, whose coastal explora-

tions as far south as the mouth of the river Plate are also shown. The Pacific coastline has been added later.

In North America the 'land of the Codfish' (*terra de los bacalos*), so named by the Portuguese who followed Sebastian Cabot to the fishing grounds off Labrador and Newfoundland, is set near the island of Seven Cities which has been transferred by the map-maker from the Atlantic Ocean to the American mainland. The origin of the Seven Cities legend was related by the globe-maker Martin Behaim in 1492. 'In A.D. 734 when the whole of Spain had been won by the African Heathen the above island Antilla called Seven Cities was occupied by an archbishop from Oporto in Portugal and six other bishops . . . who fled thither from Spain. In 1414 a ship from Spain got nearest to it without danger'.

As a spur to geographical exploration in the sixteenth century, legends of vast natural deposits of gold, and jewel-laden native empires cannot be overestimated. One of the most influential beliefs, current in Spain from the 1530s, was that the Kingdom of 'El Dorado', quite literally the 'gilded-one', lay somewhere between the rivers Amazon and Orinoco in South America. The discovery of the Aztec and Inca kingdoms only strengthened the Spaniards' conviction that other wealthy civilisations must exist. This was reinforced by accounts given by the coastal Indians of Guiana about a people who were skilled 'in many trades, and very rich in gold which they dedicate to the numerous sanctuaries which they use in hills and mountains'. The tale told by the Indians to the credulous and acquisitive Spaniards was in fact partly true, although exaggerated. During the fifteenth century the Chibcha nation of the central Colombian plateau above Bogotá had indeed held an annual religious ceremony on the shores of Lake Guatavita. Their chief had coated his body with gold dust and bathed in the lake while

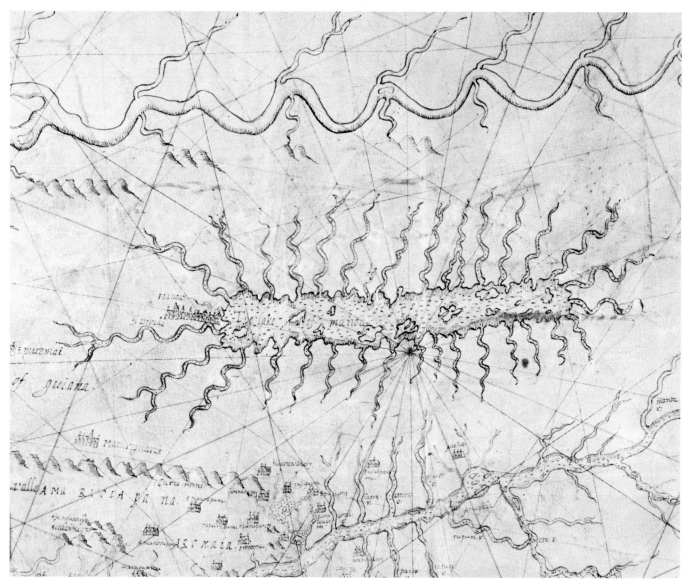

36   *Eldorado drawn on a map by Sir Walter Ralegh, c.1595*

his followers threw jewels and gold into it. In 1535 the lake was discovered, but the amount of gold recovered was disappointingly small. Far from destroying the legend, this merely meant that the realm of El Dorado slipped further inland into an unknown range of mountains high in the Orinoco basin. Thence Sir Walter Ralegh set sail in 1595 to discover 'a better Indies for her Majestie then the King of Spaine has any'. The Spanish governor Antonio de Berrio, who had himself searched for El Dorado in the 1580s, was convinced, and convinced Ralegh, that the kingdom lay by a very great lake surrounded by hills and mountains. His general, Domingo de Vera, had further reported in 1593 that he had been told by Indians inland from the Orinoco that 'not a day's journey off . . . there were as many Indians as would shadow the sun and so much gold that all the plain would contain it'. On his return from the 'Discoverie of the large rich and bewtiful empire of Guiana' Ralegh recorded on a map in his own hand the location of the lake and city of Manoa, called by the Spaniards 'El Dorado' (**36**). Although the map is unsigned it has been reliably attributed to Ralegh from a comparison with the maps drawn in Ralegh's common-place book (B. L. Additional MS 57555). Ralegh's own explorations had been confined to the Orinoco, but he too believed that the golden city existed.

Under these receptive conditions, which continued to prevail well into the nineteenth century, it is not perhaps surprising that the opportunity to practise deceptions was occasionally taken. In 1708 an article was printed in the *Monthly Miscellany of Memoirs for the Curious* which puported to be a letter from a Spanish Admiral named Bartholemew de Fonte giving an account of his travels in search of the North-West Passage from the Pacific to the Atlantic. The amusing nature of the letter had many of the hall-marks of a work by Defoe but, even so, the account succeeded in hoaxing geographers, notably the usually sceptical J. N. De L'Isle. In 1752 he and his brother-in-law Philippe Buache drew a map showing these new discoveries entitled 'Carte Generale des Découvertes de l'Amiral de Fonte' which Thomas Jefferys translated into English in 1768 (**37**). The most notorious example of genuine confusion, however, is surely that which involved California. In the sixteenth century it was mapped as a peninsula but in the seventeenth and early eighteenth centuries it became an island. About 1690 Gerard Valck, the Amsterdam map-publisher, included the island on a large wall-map (**38**). An accompanying legend in Latin explains that

38 *California as an island, c.1686*

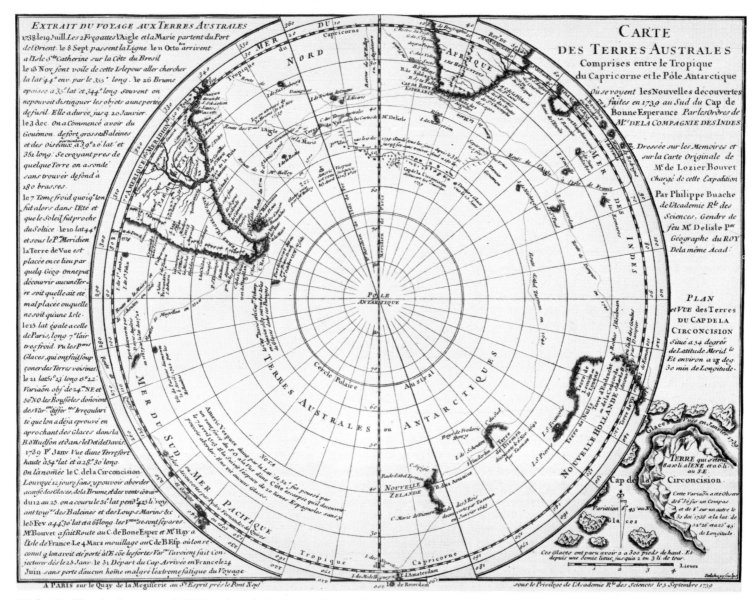

39 & 40 *The development of Philippe Buache's theory of a southern continent, 1739–1754*

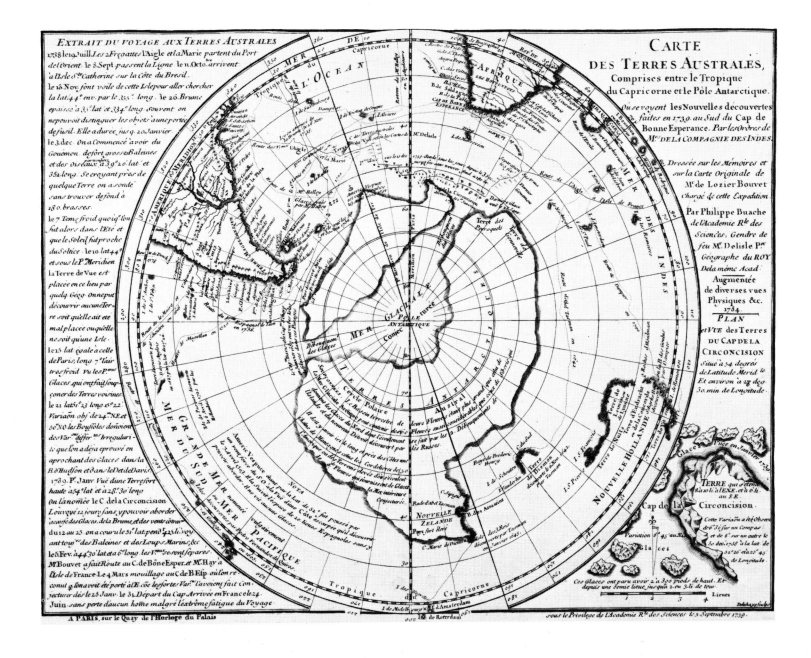

Carte des Terres Australes, Comprises entre le Tropique du Capricorne et le Pôle Antarctique.

earlier geographers had been accustomed to thinking that California was part of the continent, but that the Dutch now knew from captured Spanish charts that it was indeed an island. Valck, like his contemporary Joan Blaeu, had evidently copied his map from the one which accompanied Henry Briggs's account of the North-West Passage which was first published in *Purchas His Pilgrimes* in 1625. Briggs had seen a Spanish chart which had been captured by the Dutch in 1622. This in turn is usually thought to have been based on the journal written by Father Antonio de la Ascension who sailed with Sebastian Vizcaino in 1602 for the Californian peninsula. Father Ascension asserted that 'the Kingdom of California was separated from the provinces of New Mexico by the Mediterranean Sea of California'. As the northerly part of the gulf of California was unexplored it was easy to think that it might extend as far north as 46° and might even join the Pacific Ocean.

Strange geographical ideas and misconceptions were not confined to any one continent nor to any particular period. In 1739 Philippe Buache first expressed cartographically his theory of continental land masses in the southern hemisphere (**39**). In his map he marks the routes and discoveries of explorers who had found land in Antarctic regions. On a later state of the same map dated 1754 (**40**) he has revised it to show two hypothetical continents pivoted round the Antarctic pole. The New Zealand coasts discovered by Abel Tasman are absorbed into the larger of the two land-masses. A text aptly entitled *Soupçonnées* (Conjectures) explains Buache's ideas on the terrain of these southern lands. He informs us that they contain rivers as wide and as large as those in Siberia and mountain ranges along their coasts like the Cordilleras of America.

In Africa, too, earlier legends about the source of the river Nile in the Lakes and Mountains of the Moon were revived in the mid-nineteenth century by missionaries. These notions became confused in the 1850s when two German missionaries Jakob Erhardt and Johann Rebmann sent home tales of a great inland sea. Claudius Ptolemaeus (AD 90–168) had described in his *Geography,* first printed in 1477, how the Nile flowed from a series of lakes which in turn were filled by the melting snows from the Mountains of the Moon in East Africa. When therefore in 1848–9 Mount Kenya and Mount Kilimanjaro were discovered, native stories of a large inland lake or series of lakes became readily

acceptable to Europeans. The German map-publisher Augustus Peterman included a map showing the results of Rebmann's and Erhardt's speculations about the 'Sea of the Mountains of the Moon' in an issue of his *Geographische Mitteilungen* in 1856 (**41**). The lake of *Unyamwesi,* as they called it, forms a stout 'L' shape stretching southwards from what is now known as Lake Victoria at the Equator via Lake Tanganyika to Lake Nyasa. The missionaries seem to have unwittingly conflated reports of the three lakes into one great inland sea, the size of the Caspian. The problems of the Nile source and of this immense lake were not to be finally solved until H. M. Stanley circumnavigated Lakes Victoria and Tanganyika in 1875–6.

Geographical confusions, deliberate or otherwise, were from time to time further complicated by the cartographers' own fancies (see also **76**). One of the perks of the map-maker's and map-engraver's profession was the opportunity of immortalizing their names and those of their friends or patrons on the maps and charts they drew. In lieu of real islands or other features to label they were sometimes invented. An early English example of this tendency is to be found on the map of Ireland drawn by Baptista Boazio in 1599 and subsequently engraved by Renolde Elstracke which shows 'Elstracke's Ile' and 'Baptistes rock' off the coast of Ulster. A more extravagantly fictitious island was drawn by Captain William Hack (d.1708) in his 'Description of the Coast & Islands in the South Sea of America' first made in 1687 and re-copied by him in 1698 (**42**). In latitude 47° 40′S a piece of delightful flattery occurs when Hack devotes a whole chart to mapping Pepys's island, discovered by the pirate William Cowley in January 1684. Cowley describes the isle as 'very pleasant to the eye with many woods' and notes that along its south-west side there was a sound for about 500 ships to ride. He further opined that the island was part of the 'Sibble Dewards' (Sebald de Weert islands). Faced with this unnamed but well-described place, Hack seems to have decided to call it 'Pepys's Island' in honour of Samuel Pepys, Secretary to the Navy. He further included 'Pepys's Table Land', 'Secretaries Point' and 'Admiralty Bay' — most suitable names of the Secretary's own Atlantic isle. According to Edward Lynam, Hack, when copying Cowley's journal, even went so far as to alter the text to read 'I gave it the name of Pepys Island' which was repeated in the printed version edited by Hack in 1699.

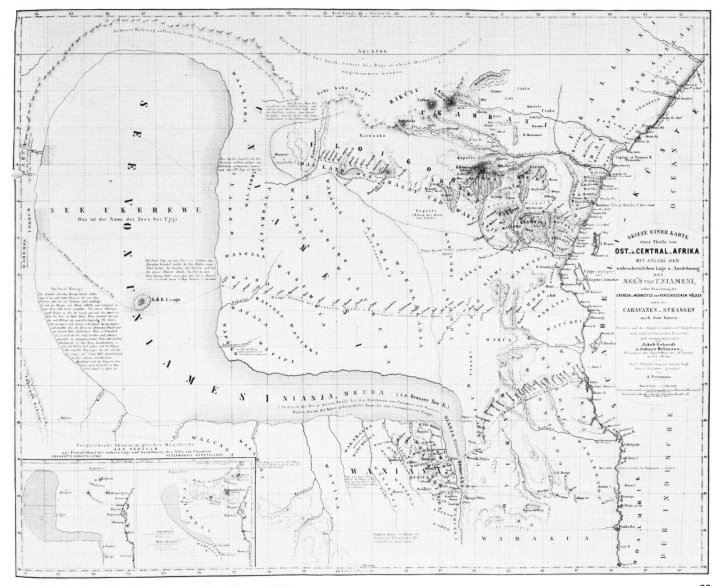

41   *The Lake of the Mountains of the Moon, 1856*

Map-makers also recorded on their maps and charts the presence of fabulous beasts, many of which under closer inspection reveal themselves as identifiable species made grotesque by the embroidered tales of travellers. Of the many maps depicting sea-monsters, perhaps the *Carta Marina* by Olaus Magnus was the most influential. First printed in 1539 on nine sheets, the map showed Scandinavia, Iceland and the north of Scotland set round the North Sea filled with dangerous maritime creatures. The map was then copied by the Italian map-publisher Antonio Lafreri and re-issued in a much reduced version at Rome in 1572 (**43**). The sea beasts are a mixture of the real and imaginary. Monster 'K' near the island of Tile (Thule) is labelled 'Monstrum 1537 visum', that is a monster sighted in 1537. In the key to the map Magnus gives fuller accounts of the various animals; 'K' is a 'Hyena the sea-hogge, a monstrous kind of fish'. 'D' is called 'Ziphius' with a long spiked snout, a 'horrible marine monster' which the geographer, Abraham Ortelius, later tried to identify as 'the sword fish which swallows the black seal at one bite'. Versions of Olaus Magnus's monsters populated and decorated the seas on charts until the mid-eighteenth century.

Similarly long-lasting are the legends and consequent depictions on maps of strange human beings. Many of these representations were derived from the descriptions given in the *Natural History of the World* written by the elder Pliny (AD 23–79) and first printed in Latin in 1469. He in turn based his accounts on the fabulous tales written down by Ktesias from Knidos who had resided as royal physician at the court of Artaxerxes Mnemon of Persia during the fourth century BC. Pliny's ideas were absorbed by most geographers of the sixteenth century, and were particularly well illustrated in the successive editions of Ptolemy's maps published by Sebastian Münster, professor at Basle, from 1540 onwards. On the Ptolemaic map of Asia a number of strange beings are placed in Scythia or part of northern Asia (**44**). Münster shows the *Anthropophagi* who feed on man's flesh and who live about the North Pole. According to Pliny 'they drinke out of the sculs of men . . . and weare the scalpes, hair and all'. Münster also depicts in the margins of the map those human beings described by Pliny in Book 7: 'In India there is a kind of men with heads like dogs . . . who in lieu of

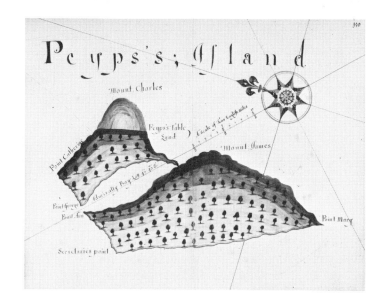

speech use to bark. Likewise there is a kind of people named *monoscelli* that have but one leg apiece. In the hottest season of the Summer they lie along on their backe and defend themselves with their foot against the Sunnes heat'. The last tribe to be shown, those with their faces below their shoulders, reappear, as do the *anthropophagi,* in the New World of America. The legends of the Old World were transferred to the unexplored continent. Sir Walter Ralegh alludes to this phenomenon in his description of Guiana where he tells of the existence of a warrior tribe with their heads below their shoulders in the Orinoco basin and also describes the fierce Amazonian women. Both these American beings are engraved on a map of Guiana published by Jodocus Hondius at Amsterdam in 1599. A contemporary manuscript annotation in Dutch ('dict Ralegh') cites Ralegh as the authority for their inclusion. He in turn refers in his *Discoverie* to the classical story of a nation of Amazons living in Scythia. Ralegh however improves on the original Old World story by pointing out that it does not seem to be true that these Amazons had the right breast removed to facilitate using a bow and arrow. His Amazon on the printed map is perfectly endowed.

42 *Samuel Pepys's island, 1698*

43 *Sea monsters, 1572*

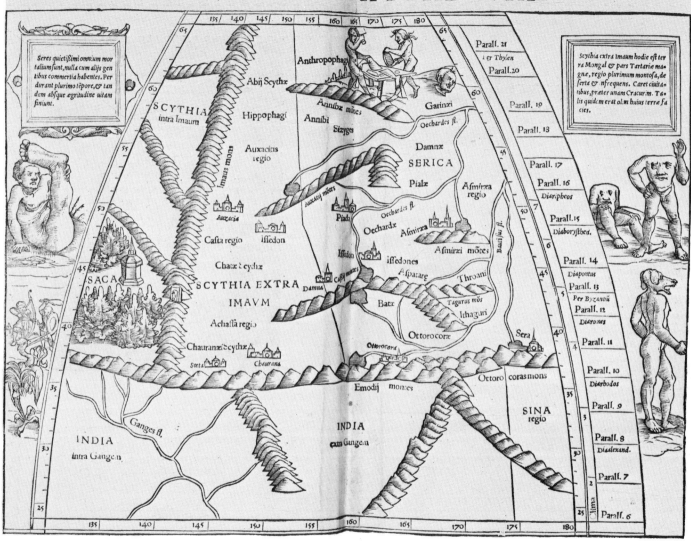

TABVLA ASIAE VIII·

SCYTHIA
intra Imaum

Abij Scythæ

Hippophagi

Auxaciis regio

Anthropophagi

Annibæ mōtes
Annibi
Sizyga

Garinæi

Oechardes fl.

Damnæ

SERICA

Pialæ

Asmiræa regio

Imaus mons

Auxacij mōtes

Piala

Oechardæ fl.

Oechardæ

Asmirra

Asmiræi mōtes

Auxacia

Iffedon

Casta regio

Iffedon

Iffedones

Casij mōtes

Asparatæ

Throani

Tagurus mōs
Ithaguri

Chatæ scythæ

SCYTHIA EXTRA

IMAVM

Damna

Batæ

SACA

Achassa regio

Ottorocoræ

Sera

Chauranæi scythæ

Soeta

Chaurana

Ottorocora

Ottoro corasmons

Emodij montes

SINA
regio

Ganges fl.

INDIA

intra Gangen

INDIA

extra Gangen

Parall. 21
1 & Thylen
Parall.20
Parall. 19
Parall. 13
Parall. 17
Parall. 16
Diaripheos
Parall.15
Diaboryfthen.
Parall. 14
Diapontus
Parall. 13
Per Byzantiū
Parall. 12
Diarones
Parall. 11
Parall. 10
Diarhodos
Parall. 9
Parall. 8
Diadexand.
Parall. 7
Parall. 6

Clima

a Detail from the engraved version of Sir Walter Ralegh's map, 1599

b A South American unicorn, c.1686

As strange human beings were transferred from the Old to the New World during the sixteenth century, so mythical land beasts assumed an American guise. The unicorn which was so often drawn on maps in areas of Asia and Africa also appears in South America, but as a distinctly South American animal — the *paco*. On the wall-map of America published by Gerard Valck at Amsterdam about 1690, a couple of one-horned woolly *pacos* or sheep are drawn, together with a curly-horned sheep. A century earlier the Dutch chronicler Linschoten had shown a pair of gazelle-like unicorns in Central India on one of the charts in his *Itinerario*, 1596.

Although the monsters continued to appear on maps, some doubt was beginning to be cast on their authenticity. Even Sebastian Münster had wondered about the existence of the monstrous races: 'The ancients have devised many peculiar monsters which are supposed to exist in India . . . However there is nobody here who has ever seen these marvels'. He was not, however, prepared to state that they did not exist, preferring to leave the question open: 'I will not interfere with the power of God, he is marvellous in his work and his wisdom is inexpressible'. His equivocal position was shared by his contemporaries who expected the world to be full of marvels but always in far-away places.

c An Indian unicorn, 1596

ASIA SECUNDA PARS TERRÆ IN FORMA PEGASI.
SEPTENTRIO.

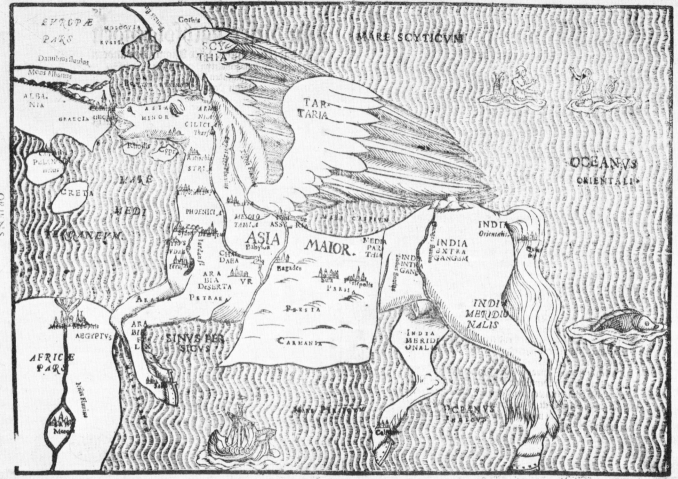

Jesus Christus magnus ille Bellerophontes, omnium malorum occisor ascendens Pegasum, hoc est, in Asia fontem doctrinæ aperiens Solimos vicit, & chimæram interfecit horribile monstrum quod flammas evomens caput & pectus Leonis habuit, ventrem autem Capræ, & caudam Draconis, hoc est, Superavit ac Interfecit filius antiquum illum Draconem Diabolum, sublato peccato morte ac inferno.

46   *Asia in the shape of Pegasus*

4 Man and Beast

While fabulous beasts were still to be seen on maps of the New World, more familiar creatures were appearing on some maps of the Old. They were not always in the form of small vignettes, placed in blank spaces for decoration; sometimes they even absorbed whole continents, reducing the maps to relative insignificance.

Among the earliest examples of this kind of map are those depicting Europe as a woman. First produced by Joannes Bucius in 1537, this theme became very well known through the versions which appeared in Münster's *Cosmography* between 1544 and 1628, and in Heinrich Bünting's *Itinerarium Sacrae Scripturae*. The design has west at the top of the map, with Spain as a crowned head, Italy the right arm, and Denmark the left. Eastern Europe forms the skirt of her dress, the hem of which runs northwards from Greece. It has been suggested that the figure is not a woman, but the Emperor Charles V. The robes are sketchy enough to be either female or imperial, and the argument is based on the idea that Spain was at the time the 'crown of Europe'; the sceptre in the left hand, which reaches the British Isles, becomes a symbol of the alliance between Charles V and Henry VIII.

Bünting produced not only a version of Europe as a woman, but two further woodcut maps, in both of which the true shape of the land is considerably distorted. *Asia secunda pars terræ in forma Pegasir* (**46**) shows Asia in the shape of a winged horse, which is drawn fairly realistically, so that the shape of Asia has to be adjusted: the Caspian Sea lies horizontally between the wings and the saddle, and modern India is the off hind leg. His third map shows the world as a clover-leaf (**47**). Each of the three continents of the Old World forms a section, with Jerusalem in a circle in the middle. England and Scandinavia appear separately at the northern edge of the map, and America, the New World, can be seen in the south-west corner.

In later designs of this kind the map is less often distorted. Sometimes it is drawn quite straightforwardly, and surrounded by further decoration: this is the case with Oronce Finé's map of the world enclosed in a fool's cap (**45**), before 1580, and Philipp Eckebrecht's *Noua Orbis Terrarum* in which the world is framed by a double-headed eagle.

By far the most popular of the animal maps has always been the *Leo Belgicus*. This particular conceit was originally devised by Baron Michael von Eytzinger in 1583, to illustrate his history of the Low Countries, *De Leone Belgico*. Belgium did not then exist as a separate entity, but formed part of the seventeen provinces of the Netherlands, which covered the whole lowland area. The map, which shows all seventeen provinces enclosed in the form of a lion, is not distorted in any way; the beast's outline is neatly superimposed, with great dramatic effect. The lion is half standing, his right forepaw raised, facing east with mouth open and tongue protruding. His spine follows the coastline from north-east to south-west.

Both book and lion proved immensely popular, and reappeared in several editions. Soon others began to copy the idea. Some kept closely to Eytzinger's design, but others adapted the idea to suit their own fancy. Famiano Strada's version was to become one of the best known: his map was similar to Eytzinger's but with the proportions of the lion slightly altered, and the raised forepaw resting on a shield. In 1611 Cornelis Jansson introduced a new variation, by altering the orientation so that west was at the top of the map, and designing a lion passant facing south-west.

In 1598 Joannes van Doetichum had produced a very close copy of Eytzinger's lion, down to the shields of the seventeen provinces scattered over the appropriate areas. Nearly all the provinces bore some

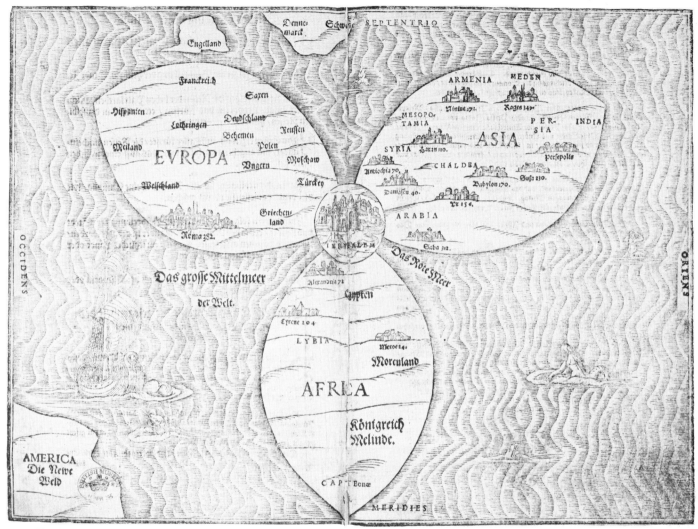

47 *The Old World as a clover-leaf*

kind of lion on their arms, so the design of the Leo Belgicus was appropriate as well as attractive. Van Doetichum's version had an extremely elaborate border incorporating the portraits of thirteen Governors of the Netherlands. Claes Jansz. Visscher reissued it in 1650 (**48**), updating the coats of arms and adding two further portraits. In 1656 (**49**) he reissued the Jansson version, with the lion passant. These were not Visscher's only Leones Belgici: as early as 1609 he had produced a variation showing the lion sitting down, its raised forepaw resting on a sword; and in 1633 a lion rampant carrying a scimitar. The idea of the Leo Belgicus was indeed so popular that further versions, in several styles, continued to be published as late as the beginning of the nineteenth century.

In 1761 a lady made her appearance on a map of the Americas. This time there can be no doubt of her sex; her features are unmistakably feminine. She forms part of a large symbolic map of the Spanish Empire by D. Vicente de Memije (**50**). East is at the top; the lady's crown is inscribed with the names of parts of Spain, while above her head a dove spreads peace and light from Rome. The Americas lie across her body, with Mexico roughly at waist level; shipping routes to and from the west form the folds of her skirt.

One of the most elaborate 'human maps' is to be found in Olof Rudbeck's *Laponia Illustrata* of 1701 (**51**). This is an account of the author's travels through Lapland, with descriptions of the countryside and wild life. One of the people he comes across is a ferryman, whose appearance reminds him irresistibly of Charon, the ferryman of the Styx: 'he put me in mind of what has been affirm'd by some Modern Authors of the Shape or whole extent of the *Baltick* Sea, to represent the posture of a Gyant, which, if taken with some grains of allowance, may perhaps challenge the same probability, as the Representations made by some Geographers of other Countries; as of *Europe,* like a *Virgin*; of *Holland,* like a *Lyon, &c.* Take then this vast Tract of our *Baltick* Sea . . . you will find it to represent in an exact Map, the shape of an Old Gyant bending his Head forward, with a crooked Back'. With various learned philological comments, Rudbeck goes on to explain all the details of his giant: his form, his clothing, even his boat, his staff and his passage-money. 'For the Privy parts you must take Balleron, Kokor and Aland, famous for its dangerous rocks', and further on, 'we will not leave our *Gyant* without a Cloak, to cover part of his Nakedness; the several Isles, Rocks

50 *The Spanish Empire as a queen*

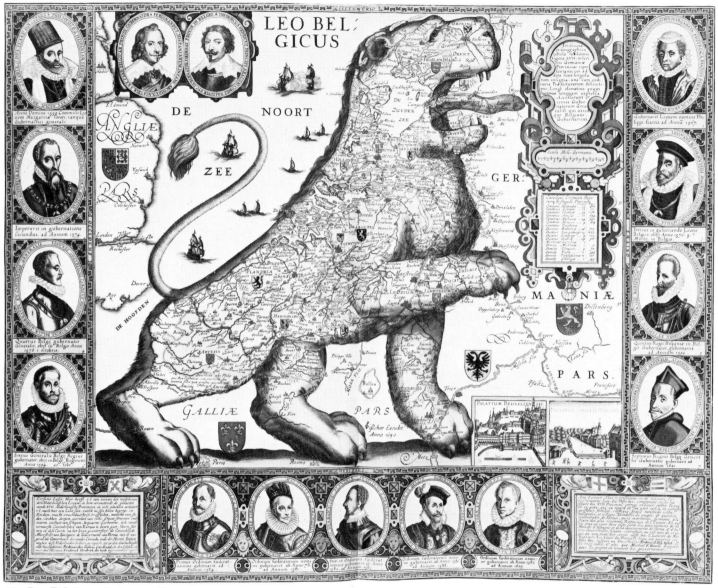

48 *Leo Belgicus, facing north-east*

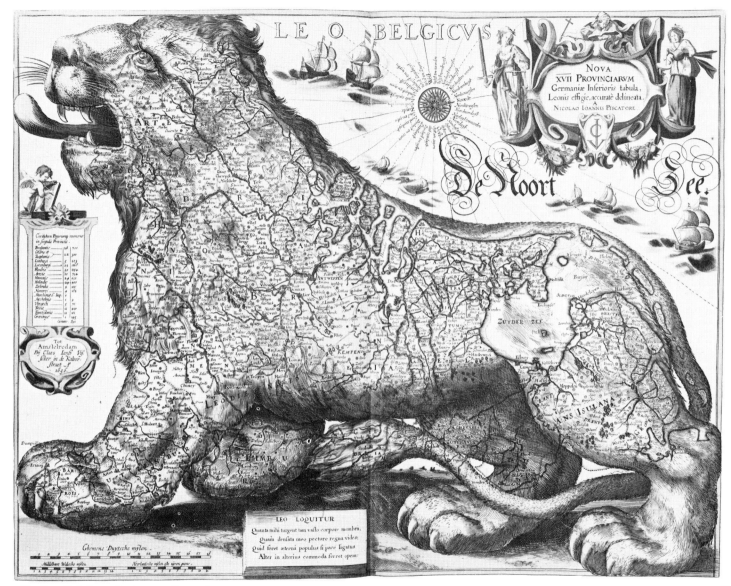

49 *Leo Belgicus, facing south-west*

51 *The Baltic in the shape of Charon*

and Capes on the Western Shoar of the *Baltick Sea* . . . seem to be placed there for that purpose, and *Schonen* instead of a buckle to fasten the Cloak on one side'.

By the end of the eighteenth century, humorous maps of this kind were appearing as separate publications rather than as illustrations accompanying a serious text. In 1795 Bowles and Carver were advertising several hundred different prints for sale, mostly of moral or humorous subjects — among others they were offering Hogarth's *Marriage-a-la-Mode* series. Two of the latest additions to their catalogue at this time were *Geography Bewitched! or, a droll Caricature Map of England and Wales* (**52**) and a companion *Map of Scotland* (**53**), each costing 6d plain or 1s coloured. England and Wales are in the shape of a cheery, beer-drinking, pipe-smoking fellow sitting on a large fish, whose open mouth is the mouth of the Thames and whose tail is Cornwall; Scotland is represented as a hunchback clown sitting on a cushion. There is no reason to suppose that any specific satire was intended by either of these pictures; they were intended simply for amusement, the shapes having been suggested by the coastlines. Hugh Hughes's *Dame Venodotia, alias Modryb Gwen* (**54**) at first sight appears to be very much the same sort of map. North Wales is shown as a barefooted old woman, leaning forward under the weight of the sack she is carrying on her back. As you look at her, however, other shapes begin to appear: goats, dogs and rabbits are all hidden in the shadows of her clothing, and the sack is discovered to be a young lady in a ball-gown.

Later in the nineteenth century political cartoon maps came into vogue. One of the first of these was *The Evil Genius of Europe* (**55**), published in 1859. The map shows Italy and the land immediately to the north. Part of the otherwise greyish lithograph is tinted pink, giving prominence to the hidden figure of a man who is trying to pull on the 'boot' of Italy back to front. Beneath the title of the map is the legend: 'On a careful examination of this Panorama the Genius will be discovered struggling hard to pull on his Boot. It will be noticed, he has just put his foot in it. Will he be able to wear it?' The 'Evil Genius' in question is Napoleon III, who in December 1858 had signed a treaty with Piedmont to provoke war with Austria and drive her out of the parts of Italy she then occupied. Napoleon was successful, and so for the time being was able to 'wear the boot'; he was to find it rather

Geography Bewitched!
or, a droll Caricature MAP of ENGLAND and WALES.

London, Printed for Bowles & Carver, No.69 St. Pauls Church Yard.

Geography Bewitched!
or, a droll Caricature MAP of SCOTLAND.

London, Printed for Bowles & Carver, No.69 St. Pauls Church Yard.

52   *Geography bewitched: England and Wales*

53   *Geography bewitched: Scotland*

uncomfortable in the future, however, when there were complications over his involvement with the papal states.

In Joseph Goggins's *Novel Carte of Europe designed for 1870* (**56**), most of the countries are shown as human figures, each in some way representative of that state's present political situation. Austria is a thin, supine figure held down by the knee of an immensely fat Prussian, the Austrians having lost the Austro-Prussian War of 1866. 'Turkey-in-Europe yawns and awakes', indicating rising nationalism in Turkey's European provinces, while Russia is shown as a bogey — her traditional rôle in late nineteenth-century Europe, mainly because she was suspected of trying to get her hands on India, which would upset the British in particular, or on the Turkish Empire, which would upset the whole balance of power in Europe.

The *Novel Carte* was immensely popular throughout Europe, and was translated into several languages. Seven years later Frederick Rose designed a map on similar principles, the *Serio-Comic War Map for the year 1877* (**57**). This became known as the 'Octopus map', for its most striking feature is a large brown octopus representing Russia. One tentacle, wounded in the Crimean War, is curled up out of the way, but the other seven are stretching out in all directions, grasping at the most accessible parts of Europe. Bulgaria is shown as a skull, in reference to the terrible Turkish massacre of the Bulgarians the previous year. Italy appears as a girl on roller-skates, playing with a puppet; the caption reads, 'Italy is ruthlessly making a toy of the Pope'. A few months later a revised version of the map appeared, with the altered caption, 'Italy is rejoicing in her freedom'. (The puppet is still identifiable as the Pope.) There seems to be no historical reason for the change — perhaps the Roman Catholic church had complained.

Rose drew a number of similar cartoons, including two of the British Isles in 1880 and a later, rather gaudy version of the Octopus map. One of the most elaborate is *Angling in troubled waters* (**58**), published in 1899. Many of the countries now appear as recognisable individuals, the largest being Tsar Nicholas in Russia, and have fishing-lines with their catches hooked on the end, occasionally with extra fish stored in nets as well. These fish represent the recent colonial advances of the various powers. John Bull for England has a netful already, and is angling for a small crocodile called Egypt, which seems to be biting. France, engrossed in the Dreyfus affair, has let Fashoda drop from her

46

54 Dame Venodotia

line: in March 1899 France had finally abandoned to Britain her claim to this colony on the Nile, which would have given her a foothold in north-east Africa. In Austria, the Emperor Franz-Josef is still mourning his Empress Elizabeth, assassinated in Geneva the previous year, and skulls in Bulgaria and Armenia again recall the Turkish massacres. Crete is dangling from a line attached to the Turk's waist: after the war between Greece and Turkey in 1897, Turkey had been forced to grant Crete autonomy, but Prince George of Greece was appointed governor 'under the suzerainty of the Sultan'. Spain is dejectedly watching her erstwhile colonies being drawn away by lines from America, to whom she had lost them in the Spanish-American war of 1898.

This particular kind of cartoon seems largely to have died out with the 1914-18 war. G. W. Bacon, who had published all Rose's maps, produced one entitled *Hark! Hark! the dogs do bark!* in 1914, with a note by Walter Emanuel. Germany is a dachshund, England a bulldog, France a poodle; the image is amusing, but the quality of the design is poor, and the accompanying text is too propagandist to be as witty as some of the captions to the earlier maps.

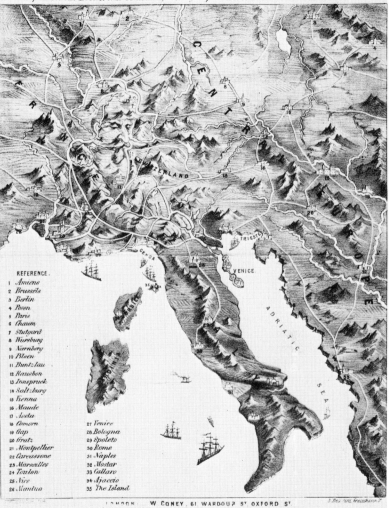

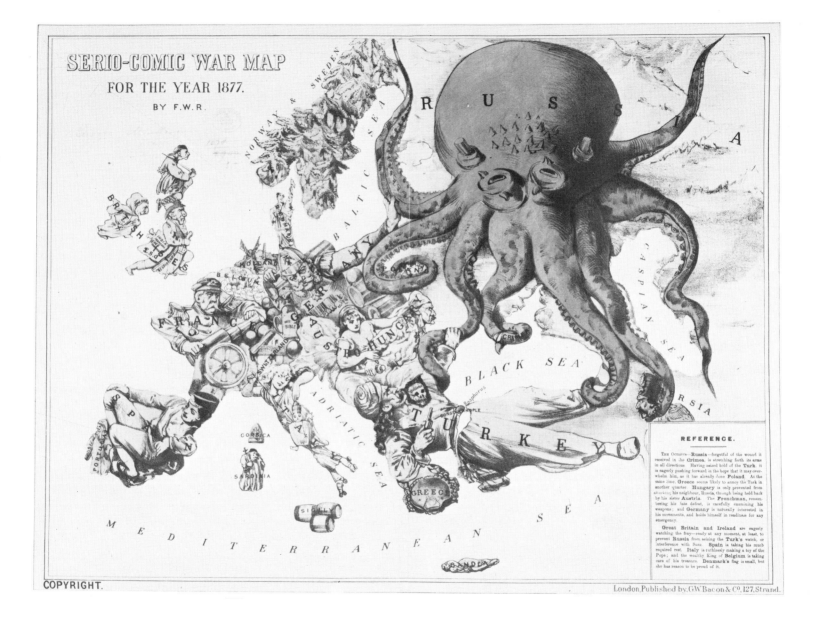

SERIO-COMIC WAR MAP

FOR THE YEAR 1877.

BY F.W.R.

REFERENCE.

THE OCTOPUS—Russia—forgetful of the wound it received in the Crimea, is stretching forth its arms in all directions. Having seized hold of the Turk, it is eagerly pushing forward in the hope that it may overwhelm him, as it has already done Poland. At the same time Greece seems likely to annoy the Turk in another quarter. Hungary is only prevented from attacking his neighbour, Russia, through being held back by his sister Austria. The Frenchman, remembering his late defeat, is carefully examining his weapons; and Germany is naturally interested in his movements, and holds himself in readiness for any emergency.

Great Britain and Ireland are eagerly watching the fray—ready at any moment, at least, to prevent Russia from seizing the Turk's watch, or interference with Suez. Spain is taking his much required rest. Italy is ruthlessly making a toy of the Pope; and the wealthy King of Belgium is taking care of his treasure. Denmark's flag is small, but she has reason to be proud of it.

COPYRIGHT.

London, Published by G.W. Bacon & Co., 127, Strand.

ANGLING IN TROUBLED WATERS

A SERIO-COMIC MAP OF EUROPE

BY
FRED. W. ROSE

AUTHOR OF THE 'OCTOPUS' MAP OF EUROPE

COPYRIGHT · TOUS DROITS RESERVES

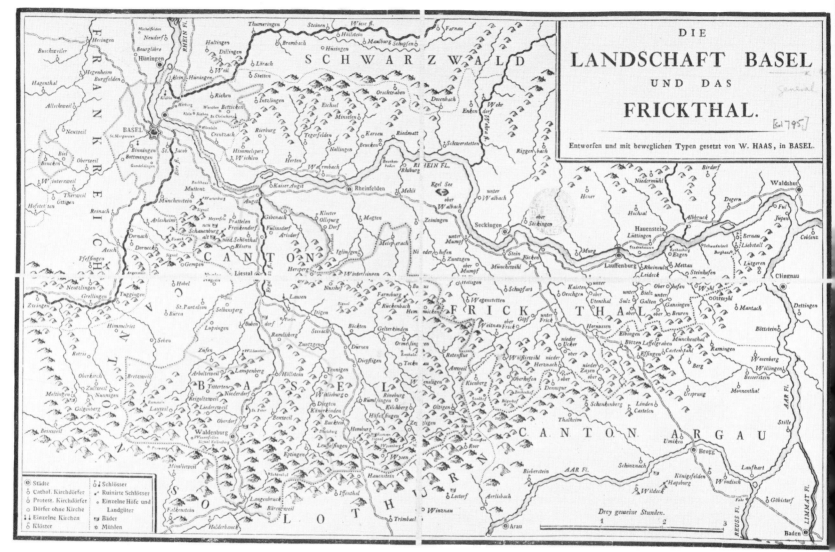

63 A typographical map of Basle

5 Curiouser and Curiouser

The religious disputes which raged in Europe during the sixteenth and seventeenth centuries found cartographical expression in the *Mappe-monde nouvelle papistique* printed in 1566 (**62**). This violently anti-papal map is filled with satirical vignettes depicting the Pope's tyrannical control of men's souls by means of his empire of sacraments, dogmas, penances and other idolatrous usages. It was probably engraved by the painter and wood-engraver Pierre Eskrich, sometimes called Vase or Cruche, who worked at Lyons in the mid-sixteenth century. The author of the accompanying descriptive book entitled *Histoire de la Mappe-Monde papistique* has hidden his identity in the name *Escorche-Messes* (Burn-masses) while the printer calls himself *Chasse-Diables* (Hunt-Devils). It is not at all clear why the pseudonyms are required as the book and map were almost certainly published in the safety of Geneva. The printer seems to have been a French Calvinist refugee called François Perrin who gained a privilege on 27 November 1565 to print a 'mappemonde papale avec le livre déclaratif d'icelle'. The work is sometimes attributed to the French Calvinist leader Théodore de Bèze (1519–1605) who governed Geneva with John Calvin and who promoted, by his writings and political dealings, the cause of Calvinism in France and elsewhere. In all probability however the author was an Italian refugee Jean-Baptiste Trento who went with Perrin to Geneva in 1565. His accompanying text is dedicated to Elizabeth I of England, whose help the French Huguenots desperately needed in their fight against the Catholic league in 1566.

Of the many amusing, if vitriolic, views, the central group of figures destroying holy images (*Guerre des Images*) with ropes and hammers graphically sums up the religious wars which caught all Europe in their fever. Likewise, the depiction of the Eucharist as the 'Papal Butchers Shop' (*Boucherie*) reflects the intense antagonism Calvinists felt towards the central Roman Catholic doctrine of transubstantiation, a belief which meant that the Eucharist was regarded by Catholics as the continuing sacrifice of Christ's body on the Cross.

Before the invention of lithography at the end of the eighteenth century, maps and pictures were normally printed from engraved copper plates. The process was costly and time-consuming, so the field was open for the discovery of a cheaper way of producing results of similar quality. In the 1770s experiments began with a new method of printing maps: movable type. The idea of movable type as such was scarcely original; it had been the standard way of printing textual matter for over two hundred and fifty years. But three people saw the possibilities of adapting it to reproduce graphic matter, by introducing additional lead characters to complement the existing letters and punctuation marks. Maps were obviously the easiest kind of graphic matter to experiment with, being already liberally scattered with repetitive symbols and names. In 1774, August Gottlieb Preuschen, of Karlsruhe, produced a very simple map of Sicily from movable type. While convinced that his technique was perfectly feasible, he realized that he did not have the specialised knowledge necessary to perfect it, and sought a collaborator. He was joined in 1776 by Wilhelm Haas, a type-founder of Basle. Haas reduced Preuschen's ambitious list of 300 new characters to the 24 most essential, and set to work. The new process was not only quicker and cheaper than engraving, but easier to correct or alter. Johann Gottlob Immanuel Breitkopf, a printer of Leipzig, read of their

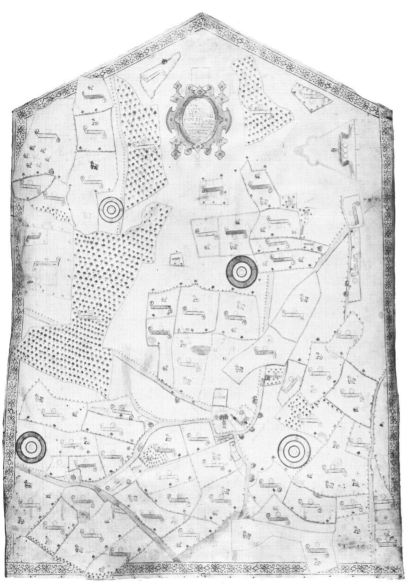

64 *Giles Burton's estate plan of Northiam*

experiments: he had been considering the possibilities of movable type for some time, but had reached the conclusion that it was not practicable for large, complex maps. A certain rivalry sprang up between them, Breitkopf implying that while he did not attempt such elaborate maps as Haas, his were much better made. There can be no doubt, in fact, that Haas's were superior. Breitkopf seems to have lacked the courage of his convictions, for of the three maps he is known to have produced two were of fictional lands — including *Das Reich der Liebe* (**66**). He was therefore able to adapt the landscape to his type characters, while Haas, who was producing ordinary topographical maps, had to do the opposite.

Interestingly enough, none of the three originators produced more than two or three maps from movable type. The person who continued working with the idea until early in the next century was Haas's son, another Wilhelm. He produced in all at least nineteen maps, nearly all straightforward geographical ones, such as *Die Landschaft Basel und das Frickthal* (**63**); but in 1790 he printed a map *Reise in dem Reich der Liebe,* closely based on Breitkopf's map of 1777.

The idea of printing maps from movable type does not seem to have caught on very widely, and the advent of the quick, cheap process of lithography removed any impetus for further experimentation. The examples that have survived, with their sometimes angular roads and rivers and their ranges of absolutely identical hills, serve as a reminder of a brief interlude in the history of map production.

Over a century earlier, in 1636, another map-maker had been employing unconventional methods in his work. Giles Burton was an estate surveyor, employed to map the lands of Thankful Frewen of Northiam in East Sussex. Thankful's father, John Frewen, had been rector of Northiam, and during his lifetime he had managed to acquire approximately 148 acres of land and woods in Northiam and in the adjoining parish of Beckley. He also owned '30 acers more or less' in Newenden and Sandhurst in Kent. All this property, as well as the house, barn, two gardens and two orchards next to Northiam churchyard, were left to Thankful on his father's death in 1629. Giles Burton was therefore faced with a considerable cartographic problem, which he succeeded in solving most ingeniously. In his plan (**64**) he shows the position and size of the fields, but ignores their relationship to the surrounding countryside, thus enabling himself to contain them

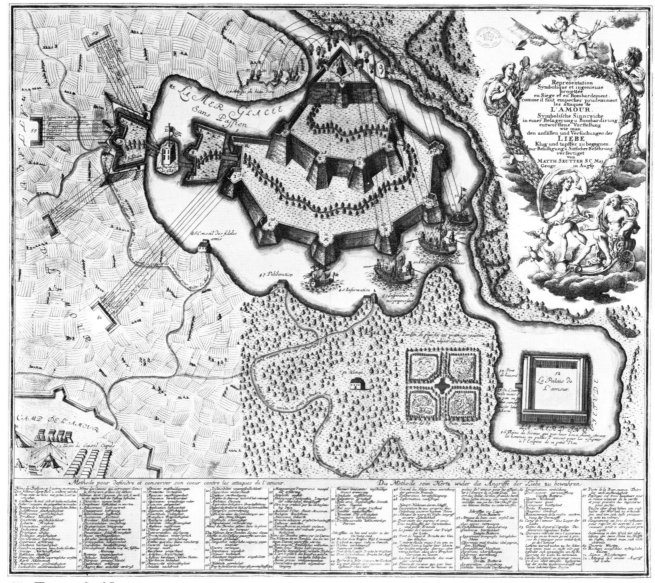

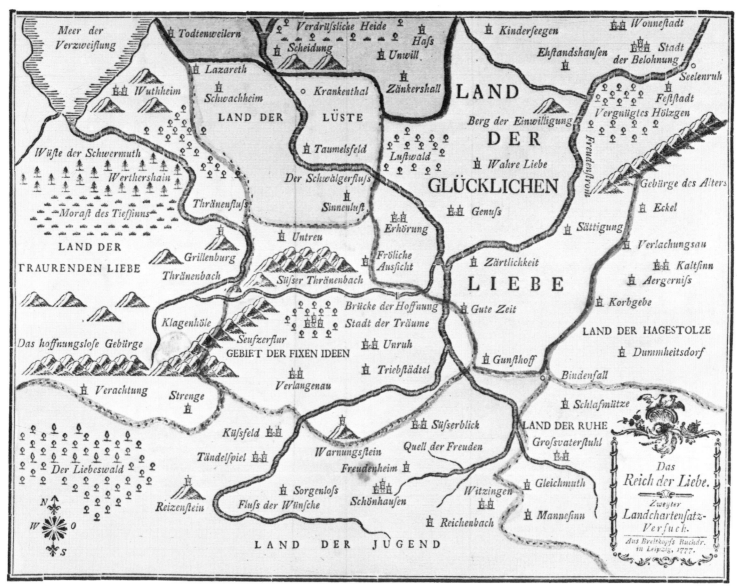

all on one piece of vellum. Each field and meadow has its own compass rose for orientation. As on his other surviving estate plans, Burton shows cows, sheep and horses by means of a die-stamp: each animal seems to have been hand-stamped on the map rather than to have been drawn by hand. Perhaps he considered the amount of estate work he undertook merited mechanical aid in the depiction of the herds and flocks of the various landowners!

In spite of Thankful Frewen's christian name, he was not a Puritan as his father was. Burton shows him standing outside his house dressed in the usual attire for a country gentleman of the period. Indeed, he was a supporter of the Laudian régime; he presented a carved oak communion table and altar-rail to the church, and died as a Royalist exile abroad.

LOVE MAPS

Love and marriage have always been among the most popular subjects for invented lands, especially in France. The famous medieval courtly romance, *Le Roman de la Rose,* is set in an allegorical landscape: a young man follows the river (of life) and finds a garden (courtly society). The allegory continues with descriptions of particular parts of the garden. More obvious symbolism was used by Madeleine de Scudéry in her novel *Clélie,* with its famous description of the 'Carte de Tendre': a land with three rivers called Inclination, Estime, and Reconaissance, and towns and villages such as Sincérité, Billet doux, and Indiscretion.

Maps have treated the subject in a variety of ways. One particularly lavish example is Matthias Seutter's *Representation Sÿmbolique et ingenieuse projettée en Siege et en Bombardement, comme il faut empecher prudemment les attaques de L'Amour* (**65**), of about 1730. This is in the allegorical tradition of the *Roman de la Rose,* but the sentiments behind the symbolism have been somewhat altered. Instead of the youth striving to attain the love of his lady, man is shown constantly on guard against the attacks of love. His central fortress, set in a passionless frozen sea, is under siege from the fair sex, being bombarded by beauty, simplicity, languishing looks, and other feminine virtues and wiles. The defence replies with volleys of prudence, industry, and experience. The palace of Love is also surrounded by sea; to enter it is easy, but few may depart without leaving their liberty

67 *Matrimonial Map*

69 *Cartographical conventions*

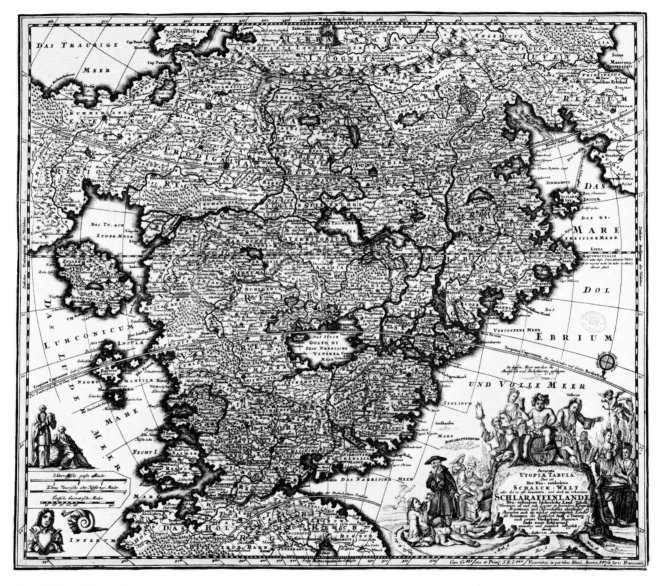

70 Schlaraffenland

behind. The fortress, on the other hand, is entered by the bridge of wisdom. Set at a little distance is the Camp of Love with the tents of General Cupid, settled in for as long a siege as may prove necessary.

By contrast, J. G. I. Breitkopf in 1777 printed a map of the kingdom of love, *Das Reich der Liebe* (**66**), with a brief explanatory text. The pilgrim sets out from the Land of Youth, in which are the sources of the rivers of Wishes and Joys. At the border of the land he comes across the Stone of Warning. There are six other lands where his travels may lead him, such as the Land of Unhappy Love, with the Desert of Melancholy and the River of Tears, and the Land of Desires, beyond which lies a no-man's-land containing the towns of Separation and Hatred, and the Heath of Vexation.

For an English view of the matter there is the *Matrimonial Map* (**67**), published in London in about 1820. Here the traveller is sailing on the Great Ocean of Love, and must take care to avoid such hazards and distractions as the Whirlpool of Impetuosity, the Floating Isles of Flattery, and the Rocks of Jealousy. He must steer a course clear of the northern land-mass, where lie the Great Barbarian Desert and the Mountains of Avarice, and head east towards St Brides Bay. Here he will find the Temple of Hymen and the Fort of Felicity, 'commanding a fine view of the Gulf of Sincerity'. The mainland, once reached, is not without its dangers: 'The source of *Inclination River* has never been rightly ascertained, travellers differing very much in this respect. The Amour, a branch of the same, is dangerous, and in some parts not fordable; on the banks have been found the *Slow Worm* and *Scorpion*; this renders it dangerous, although the scenery around is very romantic and inviting'.

Matthias Seutter, who produced the first of these love maps, was also responsible for other curiosities. One of these is the *Mappa Geographiæ Naturalis sive Tabella Synoptica* (**69**), which represents an imaginary land with an unnaturally wide variety of physical features and political divisions. The whole map is a display sheet of cartographic conventions, giving as many different examples as possible of geographical formations and of symbols used in mapping. All the examples, from water-mill to whirlpool, are carefully labelled in Latin and German; some features, such as the islands and the archbishopric, are also translated into French or Italian, or both. A list of symbols includes some that have already been identified on the map.

Even more elaborate is Seutter's map *Accurata Utopiæ Tabula Das ist Der Neu-entdeckten Schalck-Welt, oder des so offt benannten, und doch nie erkannten, Schlaraffenlandes* (**70**). Schlaraffenland is the German equivalent of the Land of Cockaigne, the imaginary country of idleness and luxury. The best known description of it is in a poem by the sixteenth-century Meistersinger Hans Sachs, who stresses the elements of food, money and lethargy. Chickens, geese and pigeons fly around ready cooked, waiting to be eaten with a minimum of effort, and every house is surrounded by a hedge of sausage. Seutter's map expands this considerably; his Schlaraffenland becomes the land of all vice. It is made up of nineteen different countries, each the home of one particular vice, and is surrounded by four others: the kingdoms of Youth and of Old Age, Terra Sancta Incognita, and Tartari Regnum — the nether regions. Altogether these lands fill a complete hemisphere, from 360° to 540° longitude. The geography of the various countries is worked out in great detail, and is described at length in a 396-page book that was published at the same time, about 1730. The numerous place-names on the map are nearly all puns, such as Alamode, Bacchanalia and Cortisan; many of them are extremely crude. To the north is New Jerusalem, in the unknown country of the pious; to the south is the kingdom of Hell, where all the inhabitants of Schlaraffenland will eventually arrive.

FROM WITCHES TO ELEPHANTS

The whimsy of the map-maker sometimes reveals itself in the most unexpected places. In 1749 Homann's heirs published an attractive perspective view of Brocken, in the Harz mountains in Germany (**75**). According to legend, Brocken was the traditional meeting-place where witches would gather on Walpurgisnacht, the eve of May Day, to hold revel with their master the devil. The summit of the mountain is known as the 'Hexen Platz', or 'place of witches', and it is here that the engraver has added a couple of small black dancing figures. Others are flying through the air on broomsticks and goats to join them. Apparently not everyone approved of his little pleasantry, for he found it necessary to add an inscription to the plate explaining that the witches were not to be taken too seriously; the addition is dated Walpurgis-Tag, 1751.

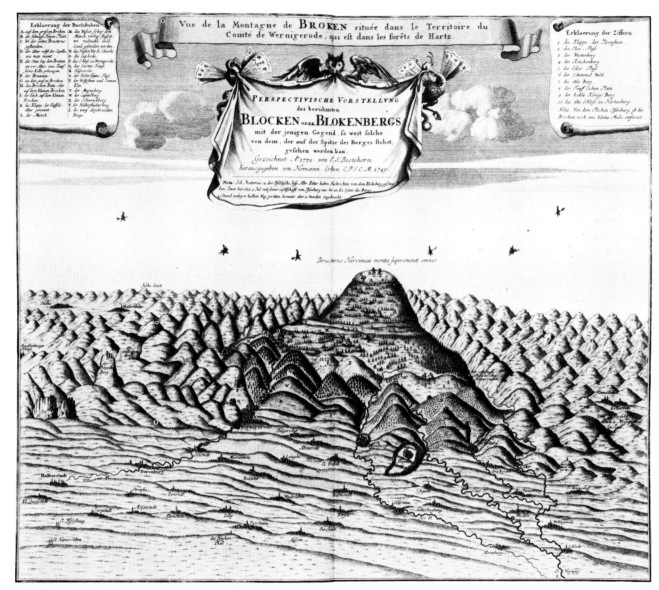

75   *View of Brocken, with witches*

Official maps and charts are not the most obvious places to look for evidence of the lighter side of map-making, but members of HM Forces have been known to be a little less than orthodox on occasion. An Admiralty chart of the island of Lemnos, in the Aegean Sea, provides a case in point. The story goes that one hot summer's day around the turn of the last century, a certain Captain Corry sent one of his junior officers out to survey a group of hills to the south-west of Mudros Bay. The young man did not particularly care for the task, and chose a somewhat unusual method of relieving his feelings. When he turned in his report, four of the hills had been named, in order, Yam Hill, Yrroc Hill, Eb Hill and Denmad Hill. No-one, apparently, saw any reason to doubt the authenticity of these suitably foreign-sounding names, and together with other more reliable survey information they were duly included in the next revision of the Hydrographic Office's chart of Port Mudros, in May 1903. There they have remained, and may still be seen on British Admiralty Chart 1661, recording the officer's wish; for if each name in turn is reversed, his hopes for Captain Corry's future are revealed.

It was the turn of the Army in 1923, when a group of young sappers were surveying an inaccessible part of Africa. At the end of a hard day's work under the tropical sun, a single hill remained to be plotted onto the plane table. The men were eager to return to base; it occurred to one of them that it was only a little hill, and could easily be filled in, by the eye of faith and with a little imagination, in the drawing office. The suggestion was generally approved, and work abandoned for the day. Later they cut out the picture of an elephant from a magazine, fixed it to their map and drew round it, creating form lines for the hill they had not surveyed. Like the names on Lemnos, the elephant escaped notice; and it too may still be seen today, in the north-west corner of sheet 17 of Africa [Gold Coast] 1:62,500 (**76**).

Cartographers do not change. Nearly two hundred years earlier, Swift had commented drily:

> 'So Geographers in *Afric*-Maps
> With Savage-Pictures fill their Gaps;
> And o'er unhabitable Downs
> Place Elephants for want of Towns'.

List of Exhibits

Items starred are illustrated in the text

* 1 Du Val, Pierre: Le jeu du monde. Paris, 1645.
      BL 999.(27)
* 2 Du Val, Pierre: Le jeu de France pour les Dames. Paris, 1652.
      BL 14425.(1)
* 3 Jefferys, Thomas: The Royal Geographical Pastime: Exhibiting a complete tour round the world. London, 1770.
      BL 950.(22)
  4 Wallis, John: Wallis's Tour through England and Wales. London, 1794.
      BL Maps C.24.b.19
  5 Wallis, Edward: Wallis's New Railway Game. London, c.1838.
      BL Maps 6.aa.42
* 6 Spooner, William: The Travellers; or, A Tour through Europe. London, 1842.
      BL Maps 197.b.35
* 7 Wallis, Edward: Wanderers in the Wilderness. London, c.1845.
      BL 785.d.41
* 8 Evans, Smith: The Crystal Palace Game. London, c.1854.
      BL Maps 28.bb.7
  9 Geographia: Buy British. London, 1932.
      BL Maps 6.d.45
  10 Teetotum, travellers and counters. 19th century.
      Lent by the Hannas Collection
  11 Spilsbury, John: The World. London, c.1772.
      Lent by the Hannas Collection
*12 Darton, William, jun.: A New Map of Africa. London, 1818.
      BL Maps 162.p.1
  13 Chichester, Francis: Shakespeare's Country. London, c.1949.
      Lent by Mrs G. Hill
  14 Barbié du Bocage, J. G.: Atlas: Amérique Septentrionale, etc. Paris, c.1875.
      BL Maps C.21.f.1

  15 Atlas Patience. German, c.1845.
      Lent by the Hannas Collection
*16 A Brief Description of England and Wales. London, c.1773.
      BL Maps 197.a.12
  17 Rongeat, A.: Amusing and Instructive Geography. London, c.1846.
      BL Maps 1.aa.4
  18 Mogg, Edward: Mogg's Dissected Globe. London, 1812.
      Lent by the Hannas Collection
  19 Miniature terrestrial globe. 19th century.
      Lent by the Hannas Collection
*20 Stokes, William: Stokes's Capital Mnemonical Globe. London, 1868.
      BL Maps 7.b.1
  21 Atlas of the British Empire, reproduced from the original made for Her Majesty Queen Mary's doll's house. London, 1924.
      BL Maps C.7.a.26
*22 Holbein, Ambrosius: Utopia. *In:* More, *Sir* Thomas, *Utopia.* Basle, 1518.
      BL 713.f.1.(1)
  23 Map of the imaginary Southern Continent. *In:* Hall, Joseph, *Mundus alter et idem.* London, c.1605.
      BL 684.d.5
*24 Wallis, John: Pilgrim's Progress Dissected. London, 1790.
      BL C.110.c.20
*25 A Map of Brobdingnag. *In:* Swift, Jonathan, *Gulliver's Travels.* London, 1726.
      BL 12612.d.23
  26 Knox, R. A.: Map of Barsetshire. *In: The London Mercury,* February 1922.
      BL P.P.5939.bp
*27 Stevenson, R. L.: Treasure Island. *In:* Stevenson, R. L., *Treasure Island.* London, 1884.
      BL 12654.cc.16

28 Shepard, Ernest: Map of the River. *In:* Grahame, Kenneth, *The Wind in the Willows.* London, 1931.
BL 12837.cc.23

29 Shepard, Ernest: Map of Pooh Corner. *In:* Milne, A. A., *The World of Pooh.* London, 1958.
BL 12841.d.1

30 Spurrier, Steven: General map. *In:* Ransome, Arthur, *Swallows and Amazons.* London, 1953.
BL 12836.aa.5

31 Tolkien, J. R. R.: Thror's Map. MS. *c.*1935.
Lent by the executors of the late Professor J. R. R. Tolkien

32 Edwards, Peter: The Rev. W. Awdry's Railway Map of the Island of Sodor. London, 1971.
BL 1296.(1)

33 Sleigh, Bernard: An Anciente Mappe of Fairy Land newly discovered and set forth. London, 1918.
BL L.R. 270.a.46

*34 Ocean-chart. *In:* Carroll, Lewis, *The Hunting of the Snark.* London, 1876.
BL 11640.h.16

*35 A map of the Atlantic showing North and South America in an atlas usually attributed to Vesconte Maggiolo of Genoa, *c.*1508.
BL Egerton MS 2803

*36 A map of northern South America attributed to Sir Walter Ralegh *c.*1595.
BL Additional MS 17940a

37 Jefferys, Thomas: A General map of the discoveries made by Admiral de Fonte. *In:* Drage T. S., *The Great Probability of a North West Passage.* London, 1768.
BL 569.f.10

*38 Valck, Gerard: America. Amstelodami *c.*1686.
BL Maps C.5.a.1

*39 Buache, Philippe: Carte des Terres Australes. Paris, 1739.
BL K.Top. IV.59

*40 Buache, Philippe: Carte des Terres Australes. Paris, 1754.
BL K.Top. IV.60

*41 Erhardt, J. and Rebmann, J.: Skizze Einer Karte eines Theils von Ost-u. Central America. Gotha, 1856.
BL P.P. 3946

*42 Hack, William: Peyps's Island. *In:* Description of the Coast & Islands in the South Sea of America, 1698.
BL K. Mar. VIII.16

*43 Magnus, Olaus: O. M. Gottus Upsalensis . . . septentrionalium suarum partium . . . Europae . . . geographiam . . . in hicem proferre . . . 1572.
BL Maps C.7.e.2.(19)

*44 Münster, Sebastian: Tabula Asiae VIII. *In:* Claudius Ptolemaeus, *Geographia.* Basilae, 1540.
BL Maps C.1.c.2

45 Finé, Oronce: 'Fool's cap' map of the world. French, 16th century.
Lent by the Bodleian Library

*46 Bünting, Heinrich: Asia secunda pars Terrae in forma Pegasir. [Magdeburg, 1585?]
BL 46820.(171)

*47 Bünting, Heinrich: Die gantze Welt in ein Kleeberblat. [Magdeburg, 1585?]
BL Maps C.26.e.5

*48 Visscher, Claes Jansz.: Leo Belgicus. Amsterdam, 1650.
BL Maps C.9.d.1.(6)

*49 Visscher, Claes Jansz.: Leo Belgicus. Amsterdam, 1656.
BL Maps C.9.d.1.(7)

*50 Memije, Vicente de: Aspecto Symbolico del Mundo Hispanico. Manilla, 1761.
BL K.Top. CXVIII.19

*51 Rudbeck, Olof: Map of the Baltic in the form of Charon. *In:* Nora Samolad, sive Laponia Illustrata. Uppsala, 1701.
BL 432.b.22

*52 Dighton, Robert: Geography Bewitched! or, a droll Caricature Map of England and Wales. London, 1795.
BL Maps 54.a.26/1

*53 Dighton, Robert: Geography Bewitched! or, a droll Caricature Map of Scotland.
BL Maps 54.a.26/2

*54 Hughes, Hugh: Dame Venodotia, alias Modryb Gwen. Carnarvon, *c.*1860.
BL 6096.(12)

*55 The Evil Genius of Europe. London, 1859.
BL 1078.(24)

56 Goggins, Joseph: Novel Carte of Europe, designed for 1870. Dublin, 1870.
BL 1078.(27)

*57 Rose, Frederick: Serio-comic War Map for the year 1877. London, 1877.
BL 1078.(35)

*58 Rose, Frederick: Angling in Troubled Waters. London, 1899.
BL 1078.(38)

59 The Great World. *In: A Geographical and Historical Account of the Great World.* London, 1829.
BL T.1267.(6)

60 L'Empire de la Poésie. *In: Le Nouveau Mercure Galant,* January 1678.
BL P.P.4482

61 Hack, William: Chart of the island of Ireland, one of the Bermudas. 1694.
BL Additional MS 5415.g.14

62 Trento, J. B.: Mappemonde nouvelle papistique. Geneva, 1566.
BL C.160.c.7

*63 Haas, Wilhelm: Die Landschaft Basel und das Frickthal. Basel, 1798.
BL Maps C.27.b.23

*64 Burton, Giles: Estate map of Northiam. MS, 1636.
BL M.T.6b.1.(30)

*65 Seutter, Matthias: Representation Symbolique et ingenieuse projettée en Siege et en Bombardement, comme il faut empecher prudemment les attaques de L'Amour. Augsburg, c.1730.
BL Maps C.26.f.4.(42)

*66 Breitkopf, J. G. I.: Das Reich der Liebe. Leipzig, 1777.
BL 116.1.31

*67 Matrimonial Map. [London, 1820?]
BL Tab 597.b.(16)

68 An Illustrative Map of Human Life, Deduced from passages in Sacred Writ. New York, 1842.
BL 999.(63)

*69 Seutter, Matthias: Mappa Geographiae Naturalis sive Tabella Synoptica. Augsburg, c.1730.
BL Maps C.26.f.4.(43)

*70 Seutter, Matthias: Accurata Utopiae Tabula, Das ist... des... Schlaraffenlandes Neu-erfundene lächerliche Land-Tabell. Augsburg, c.1730.
BL Maps C.26.f.4.(46)

71 Mappa Britanniae faciei Romanae secundum fidem Monumentorum perveterum depicta. *In: Stukeley, William, An Account of Richard of Cirencester.* London, 1757.
BL 577.h.25.(3)

72 Map of the lands claimed by the Lady Ivy. *In: The Famous Tryal in B. R. between Thomas Neale, Esq; and the Late Lady Theadosia Ivy.* London, 1696.
BL 515.k.21.(14)

73 Plan of St. James's Palace. *In: A full answer to the dispositions... concerning the birth of the Prince of Wales.* London, 1689.
BL Additional MS 33954 ff 55b,56

74 A standard form of map to be used upon all occasions. *In: Sykes, Sir Mark, and Sandars, Edmund, Tactics and Military Training.* London, 1902
BL 8826.aa.43

*75 Bestehorn, L. S.: Perspektivische Vorstellung des berühmten Blocken oder Blokenbergs. Nurmberg, 1749.
BL 30058.(1)

76 Gold Coast Survey 1:62, 500. Sheet 17. Accra, 1923–.
BL 65330.(25)

77 San Serriffe. Original art-work for the map published in *The Guardian* on 1 April 1977.
Lent by The Guardian

78 Homann, Johann Baptist: Geographische Universal- Zeig und Schlag-Uhr. Nuremberg, c.1760.
BL Maps C.26.f.5.(18)

79 Bridgment, Alice: England and Wales. 1870. (A sampler.)
BL Maps 196.c.16

80 Pocock, Ebenezer: A paper globe of the earth. Bristol, c.1835.
BL Maps C.3.bb.1

81 Chikyū-gi, Shintei. [A terrestrial globe, revised.] Tokyo, c.1880. (Japanese umbrella globe.)
BL Maps C.3.bb.3

82 Three Bartholomew maritime chart weights. Burslem, 1889–91.
Lent by Mr Raymond O'Shea

83 Letter opener, distributed by the Eastern Telegraph Company. London, 1898.
Lent by Mr Raymond O'Shea

84 The Ladies Travelling Fann of England and Wales. London, 1768.
Lent by the Hannas Collection

85 Five plates bearing maps of Hertfordshire, Oxfordshire, Somerset, Paris, and Rhône et Loire.
Hertfordshire plate lent by Mr Peter Walne
Oxfordshire, Somerset, Paris and Rhône et Loire plates lent by Mr Raymond O'Shea

86 A miniature terrestrial globe, mounted on a seal. Silver. German, early 19th century.
Lent by Mr Dudley K. Barnes